The Shepherd

The Shepherd

MAYANK MOHAN ARJARIYA

PAPER TOWNS
PUBLISHERS

PAPER TOWNS
PUBLISHERS

First published by
Papertowns Publishers
72, Vishwanath Dham Colony,
Niwaru Road, Jhotwara,
Jaipur, 302012

The Shepherd

ISBN Print Book - 978-93-87131-32-3

Dedicated to:
My *Guru*, Shri Aatam Swaroop Ji
My Nana *Guru*, Shri Jagdish Prasad Chaturvedi Ji
&
My Literature *Guru*, Dr. Sheelchand Paliwal Ji

Acknowledgements

I am grateful to all the characters of stories of this book, who accepted the roles assigned to them. Because these characters made me learn to love, to express it and to cherish it in full swing.

I am grateful to my mother, Mrs. Sudha Arjariya, for her unconditional love towards me, for her ever sensing ability about my troubles, for her worrying about whether I took dinner timely today or not and for being my first teacher of writing skills.

I am grateful to my father, Mr. Surendra Arjariya, for being with me when I needed him the most, for always worrying about whether I am driving safely or not and for all the support and security he provided me.

I am grateful to my wife, Smita, for being my wife and for continuous support.

I am grateful to my seniors at my employer company MPMKVVCL, Bhopal for believing in my passion for writing and keeping me a bit free to utilize the time as needed, especially DGM Mr. Zahid Aziz Khan and Manager Mr. Rakesh Tripathi.

I am grateful to the whole team of paper towns' publication for providing me the platform and for such a creative design and drafting, especially Mr. Narendra Singh for being in touch since the very start.

Prologue

We all do want to attain success in our life. Now, what does success mean to me? It's simple to throw my delivery according to plan and start planning for the next. To accept whatever results come meanwhile. The result may be according to the plan or maybe better in respect, in that case, to start working for a new goal and if the result doesn't fulfil the demands according to plan then to try again!

To understand the art of love, to gain energy by loving and to utilize the energy of the love in attaining our goals, is a great and secret process. It is great because it is related to the energy of love and it is a secret because love and goal, both attributes belong to two different worlds having different dimensions. Love is a subject of heart and goal is a subject of mind. And the things which haven't been proved by science yet, are seen as magic or secret.

Love and goal share such a great connection with each other that if I say, "Sir, you don't love the person, you actually love your goal." Well, at first you may agree or disagree with this but later you will find out the truth.

If this is the case, and people love their goal then why most of the population is not so happy?

"Sir, it's just because they are not able to convert their energy of love into desirable forms. They are just attached."

Love has such great energy that if it is handled with care then it is more than adequate to fulfil your dreams. And the opposite may be as dangerous too.

My aim to write this book was to share my experiences with the youths, who believe in power of love and positivity. Who want to utilise their energy of love in attaining their goals with fresh breath, forgetting all ups and downs related to past. All the best!

Content

Part A
Poems

Who cares!!!

The horse of my life is running so fast,
how will I ride on it?
The tree of my aim is so high,
how will I climb on it?
The goal decided by me is so far,
how will I reach there?
The answer to all the questions
I am searching somewhere.

Yes, I have the key in my mind.
it's a simple answer of such kind.

For riding on the horse, who cares!
For climbing on the tree, who cares!
For reaching the goal, who cares!
Because these tasks can be finished by the person, who dares.

The one I love...

There is someone whom I love,
but I don't know who's that?

I am searching for the one everywhere, in every person,
someday, somewhere, I'll definitely get her.
Up to now, I watched from the sight of parameters,
this was the main mistake I committed.

As the options are reducing.
my heart is beating faster and faster.
I don't know whether it is zeal to reach nearer to the one.
Or it's a fear of how I will face the one at first?

Now I forgot all the parameters,
perhaps, that's why fear ran many miles away from me.
I was unknown from the fact till now
that there is no parameter for the infinity.

Whoever you are, now I have to dare to meet you,
to talk to you, to live a real life with you.

Don't say bye...

Today, there are no words to say.
Just silence watching the way.

Don't know where it's about to go.
Now the time has come for the next part to play.
Some will be there with us again.
Some friends will go a different way.

After holding the bag on my shoulders,
just taking a view, where I used to play,
we used to eat together, in the mess,
playing cards, gossiping every day.

The beautiful face of the girl, I remember,
when I talked to her, during the first year, that day.
Her smile was so natural, so cordial,
may god keep her happy anyway.

To finish the syllabus within a few hours,
even to buy the books just before the day,
examinations were never an issue for us MANITians,
what matters is to live everything anyway.

All such moments are leaving behind,
while I am moving ahead on the way.
Just to all of you, I want to say,
I am sorry if I hurt you in any way.

Now my bus has come to receive me,
I wish to stay, but I have to go away,
Today, there are no words to say.
Just silence watching the way.

I see myself...

I see myself standing on high mountains,
with open arms.
But in the absence of you,
it's like going down.

I see myself winning over the wars of life,
with a new zeal every time.
But in the absence of you,
it's like losing everything.

I see myself crossing the oceans,
reaching nearer to the land.
But in the absence of you,
it's like drowning every moment.

But when you are with me,
in my arms.
Even If I have nothing,
it's like having everything.

I Pray...

No Matter how you've performed your role,
the world was going on, is going on and will go on.

See, see the camera has been already focused on me,
I am afraid, as the environment is filled with light around me,
and I am not ready to play my part yet,
why you're increasing my tension, by beating faster, o my heart.

I try, if I could remember some lines,
somehow I recalled, I've to pray before the Lord.
As a commander, I've to fight a battle for peace.
Suddenly I hear "Action", I've to beg blessings for triumph.

"O my Lord, I don't know, how to pray?
About the tight corners of my life, what should I say?
I've forgotten the lines of my part, I had to play,
I only know, I am completely yours and on your way."

As I finished the last line of the prayer,
a voice comes out from my heart, continues saying on,
No Matter how you've performed your role,
the world was going on, is going on and will go on.

He answers!

At dawn, on a bank of the holy river "Ganga",
I say, "O God, I want to feel your presence."
And the cold air flows touched me.

I say, "O God, I want to see you."
And the great sun rises.

I say, "O God, I want to listen to you."
And birds fly from their nests, generating lovely sounds.

I say, "O God, I want to talk to you."
And my friend calls me,
saying, "Come on, Mohan, it's time to play."

The one is you...

The one is with me when I am happy,
the one is with me when I am blue.
The one is natural, the one is honest,
the one is a friend, the one is you.

The one gives hope when life is low,
the one is a place when I've nowhere to go.
The one is innocence, the one is true,
the one is precious, the one is you.

The one does poetry, plays the guitar,
the one makes me wonder, I just become a statue.
The one sings then, and I feel the air in me,
the one is an artist, the one is you.

And the story continues on and on and on.
I stop, cause I need more and more words to express you.
The pen is begging to rest, and ink has dried,
Truly and heartily, the one is great, and the one is you.

In my heart, in my memories...

You often blame me of not remembering you,
because of daily busy life, I don't spare time for you,
but I want to say that you are always near to me,
you are always here, in my heart, in my memories.

When I keep on struggling for the golden future,
or I remember the sweet moments of my past,
you are always here, in my heart, in my memories.

When I transfer the black money of those rich people to the needy ones
and make true the great character of robin hood,
you are always here, in my heart, in my memories.

When I get flattered after seeing some beauty
or feel strange to see artistic creatures,
you are always here, in my heart, in my memories.

Just You and Me...

Weather, It's hot summer or getting wet in lovely rain.
To get together is what I want, every time just you and me.

When I dance joyfully or sit alone in a corner tight,
To talk to you, is what I want, every time just you and me.

When I, sing songs of love or cry alone, getting ignorance.
To live with you is what I want, every time just you and me.

Signs of life...

Mohan goes where there is a sign of life.
Life gets beautiful, where there is sign of love.
Love is accepted where there is a sign of devotion.
And devotion happens where Mohan loses himself.

Part B
Stories

The Princess and the Shepherd

Scene- First

Once, at the end of the first decade of the twenty-first century, I went to visit the famous *Khajuraho* temples of India. There, outside the *Matangeshwar* temple, I was resting upon a stone. After seeing me resting, some more people came and sat there. One of them said, “Now what? We have visited the temples here and our train is in the evening. I am getting bored now.” A guide came there and asked them if they are interested to know the history of those temples. But the people refused saying that they had already read about all stories in the guide book. One of them said,” Come on guys let’s play some games.” Another refused by saying, “Oh please, we are tired.” Then I interfered in their conversation and said, “I have something to share with you, if you are interested, then I can.” One said, “Are you going to tell any story?” Second said, “And that will be related to these temples.” I said, “No, I mean yes, you can say it is a story but that’s not about the history of these temples.” One said, “Oh, is that a love story?” I said, “Yes, you can say that”. All turned their faces towards me and I started, “Love can travel, even beyond the births.”

Scene- Second

She was a princess and I was a shepherd. She used to wake up early morning, just to leave her sheep to me. Although it was not her duty but still she loved to do it. The very first day of our meeting, when my father was suffering from fever that day and he asked me to go with the sheep. My duty was nothing apart from looking after the sheep while they are grazing. I agreed and reached nearby the royal garden, which was situated just behind the palace of the royal family. A beautiful girl appeared to leave her sheep to me. She smiled at seeing me and asked, "I haven't seen you before," I replied, "Because I am coming here for the first time, today my father's health is not okay." She asked again "Oh, what happened to him?"

I said, "He is suffering from fever. He will be okay by today evening".

The girl (with a cute and weird expression) – "How can you say that? Do you people practice any magic?"

I smiled and said- "No because it has happened several times. He suffers only once or twice in a year with this kind of fever. It doesn't last for more than a day. And we don't know any magic like that but the things we practice for treatment are majestic."

The girl was happy to hear that my father will be okay within a day. She left her sheep with me with a promise that she will come to receive her sheep in the evening. I left the place too and went towards the jungle. The whole day I kept on thinking about her smile. That was the first day when anything drew my attention for that much time. I was eagerly waiting for the evening so that I could return and watch her smile again while handing over her sheep. But the evening arrived very late. That day, I was surprised, why did the evening arrive so late? I decided to ask my father then. After long it was evening and I returned back to the palace. I was in a hurry, my sheep were also moving fast with me. Perhaps they had read about what was running in my mind.

I was not happy to reach there because I didn't see her where she had left her sheep to me. Another girl came to receive the sheep and we discussed the whereabouts of the girl. She laughed and told me that I was talking about the princess. I was surprised. I mean she did look like a princess but why will a princess come outside the palace to leave her sheep? Anyway, the very fact ignited eagerness in my mind to know her more. But she was a princess, so what? My mind just replied to carry on. In the evening I found my father was okay and I was happy but also a bit worried. Because how will I see her smile now onwards? I will have to persuade him for taking the duty on my shoulders. But I was not in the condition to wait for even a moment and so I asked.

"Father, I think, you must rest for some more days for you are not looking fully healthy and things may be negative if you go outside for work. I've decided to work till the day, you are fully healthy." He was not ready but after a small discussion, he agreed. Perhaps he thought I was being responsible. Yes, I was being, but for what? I didn't know.

Scene- Third

I started doing that work from that day onwards. We used to meet twice in a day, while receiving and leaving the royal sheep. I would see the morning smile of the princess and keep on thinking about her cuteness throughout the day. The very style of her, to come downwards from the stairs in the garden, to hold her sheep affectionately in her hands. I had captured almost each and every activity of her during the very short span of the time. But about a week later, my father informed me about his good health. That meant I couldn't go now onwards. I was very much worried now. Next day, my father went for duty and I couldn't stop him. I just kept on resting at home that day. To rest at home, was one of my greatest hobbies but it had turned boring. I had not felt such boredom before that day. I wished that may the princess also have the same eagerness to meet me and she asks my father about me? And who knows, she may order my father that she wants me as a shepherd now onwards. Wow, how good that would be. I was just thinking this and that, waiting for my father to return. She must have asked about my absence today, I thought.

My father came in the evening and before I could ask anything, he asked me, "Do you know the princess?"

I said, "Yes, but why are you asking like that?"

Father, "she was asking about you."

"And what did you say?" I asked.

My father replied, "Nothing just that I am okay now and ready to take over my duties again."

I said, "It's okay father, but I think you should take rest now at home or you can indulge yourself in-home activity like gardening etc. I am worried about your health for this job needs visiting the jungle throughout the day." My father understood me and handed over the duties to me after all. I said, "Thanks father." He was also happy for somehow I was taking up some responsibility.

I discussed it very briefly with the princess about how did I take over the duties of my father. She was just laughing after hearing it all. She asked with a smile, "Why did you do it? Do you really want to be a shepherd?"

I replied, "Now it doesn't matter for me whether I am a shepherd or someone else, only matters for me that whatever work I do, that must have lovely people around and I must get satisfied with the work. That's it. And this work is serving both purposes for me."

She smiled to hear my answer and handed over her sheep to me that day. I hoped she must have understood that she; herself was the lovely person, whom I was talking about. I went to the jungle and thanked the almighty to turn the situations in my favor.

Scene- Fourth

One day, after the duty, when I was resting at home, I started to play the flute, which I used to play often at evening or at dawn. My hut was situated at a walking distance from the palace. After some time, some girls came to me as if they were searching for me only and I guessed it right. One of them said, "OH! Then it's you, who plays the flute." I said yes.

She said, "You are being called by the princess, she wants to meet you."

"But I already meet her daily," I replied. She said, "But the princess doesn't know that the flute player and the shepherd, both are the same."

"Okay, then you can explain the truth before her and let me enjoy, please don't disturb me," I said.

She pleaded again, “Please come with us; otherwise the princess will not be happy with us.” I was ready and went with them. As I reached there, the princess was surprised to see me and asked, “Oh! It was you? How are you so good at playing the flute? Now tell me, are you a shepherd or a flute player?” And she smiled. I just laughed. She said, “I called you to say thanks. Because I was not feeling well since yesterday and after listening to the sweet music of the flute, I am feeling better.” I returned home after a little bit of conversation.

Just another day when I went to her palace to receive her sheep, she was looking a bit tired. The smile was not natural. Although it was there but it looked unnatural. As if she was just smiling for my sake. I sensed something wrong. But before I could have said anything, she said, “I’ll wait in the evening.” I wanted to stay there to ask what happened to her but the presence of the other people stopped me. Somehow I went to the jungle. I kept on thinking throughout the day, what could be the reason?

I was quite disturbed that day and decided to go to the priest who used to live near the small temple across the river. I didn’t wait anymore. I gathered all the sheep and ordered them to stay there. But the royal sheep didn’t understand the language. So I held the royal sheep in my hands and went across the river. Soon I reached the temple and offered my prayer, sitting on my knees. The priest came there. As soon as he saw me, he said, “She can’t survive”. I said, “But what’s her mistake?” The priest shouted, “Of course not hers but do you know what her forefathers had done?” I cried, “But she is innocent,” The priest said, “Her forefathers used to be the kings of many kingdoms, they were powerful people. But due to superstitions, they started to kill the animals. They thought that they were getting the kingdoms due to the killing of animals, not because of their power." But they were wrong and started suffering. Gradually their dynasty started to lose its existence. And today this is the only family, which survived because the princess's father opposed the animal killing and stopped it forever.

"But if they have rectified their mistake, then why the princess is bound to suffer now?" I asked. Priest, "It's happening because of the bane, given by a deer. Yes, once upon a time, her forefathers killed the whole family of a deer. At the time of death, the deer gave a bane to them that their whole dynasty will get end one day. And the princess belongs to the same dynasty after all."

I asked the priest if there is any way to save the princess for she is an innocent girl, she has kindness for the animals. She loves her sheep very much. The priest said, "That's why she survived till today, but the bane has to show its effect someday, if it isn't today, then it'll be tomorrow." I cried again, "But there must be some way to save her, please help."

The priest, "Animals are innocent and true, the bane given by them can't lose its effect. But she can survive if somehow the bane could be diverted from her to someone else and also with his/her desire."

"Divert?" I asked surprisingly.

"Yes, someone will have to die, if it is not the princess, then it may be someone else, but it has to happen. And who will want to take the bane upon him/her? It's unfair and against nature. Forget it. Also, it's dangerous too for both can lose their life if they played it even with a small mistake." After I pleaded a lot, the priest suggested an idea to me.

Scene- Fifth

I was returning back to my home with all the sheep and remembering the very idea, which was suggested by the priest. The priest had said, "I am giving a majestic fruit to you, you will have to eat it but only after one bite by the princess herself. Doing so will divert the effect of the bane upon you".

Again and again, I was looking at the fruit and thinking about the role, which was written for me by the Almighty. I kept on thinking about the fruit and made up my mind to eat it but the problem was how to persuade the princess for having a bite of the fruit? I decided to do it tomorrow for I wanted to see my father once before I die. I reached the palace, left the sheep; although the princess was waiting there for me but I hurried up and managed to leave the palace as soon as possible. The first time I felt that the princess had a lot to say to me but I was dying to meet my father that day. I reached at home with my sheep.

I left the sheep at their respective places and went to wash my face. As usual, I prepared the tea and went into the garden, where my father was waiting for the evening tea. We took places on the chairs and started a discussion. My father said to me, "My son, I am happy to see that you have become responsible now. It's a matter of proud for any father to see his son as a responsible person. To serve for the royal family is a big responsibility for they have done much favor for our family. I remember, Twenty years ago, when we used to live happily in our old home, which was situated in another kingdom near to this one. A king attacked there and seized that kingdom. He was a cruel king and his soldiers started to kill the innocent people. That day, as usual, I was in the jungle with sheep and they attacked our home. They killed your mother and looted all the money and jewelry. As soon as I reached home, they asked me to leave the place. Otherwise, they were going to kill you. I picked you up and left home as it was. After some time, I saw that our sheep followed me and they didn't stop those sheep. I was very much tired and thirsty but also worried about you and for that reason, I travelled to this place. Here, the royal family gave us shelter and since then, I am serving as a shepherd to them. Today, I am sharing it all with you because I understand that you have become mature enough to understand these things. You have to take care of all the responsibilities because as I can sense, I won't be able to live for more days from now." And he stopped. I just asked, "What does my mother look like?" My father replied, "She was very beautiful, her eyes were just like your eyes. She was a very responsible lady too. If she were alive today, she would have been very happy to see you being so responsible." I again asked, "Have you ever thought of punishing those cruel people?" My father replied, "Doing so, couldn't have returned your mother and they are powerful people, we can't fight with them, we are just ordinary shepherds. The Almighty will punish them when the time comes." I said, "Father, You are the world's best father and you played the role of a mother too for me. I am sorry for every mistake I committed," My father hugged me.

Scene- Sixth

The sun was setting and I started to prepare dinner. According to my plan, I had to go to the princess after dinner. After we took dinner, I was waiting for my father to go to sleep. Till then I talked with the sheep, "My dear sheep, you were the only ones, who were with my father during our tough days. I am going today to serve the royal family. I'll ask the princess to take revenge from the cruel king and take our old home back. I will not return here after this moment because I have to do another duty too. Take care of yourself and of my father too." I saw my father was sleeping and I left for the royal palace.

That night the moon was full. Without making any noise, I was moving further. It didn't take much time to reach there because I knew where I had to go. I started jumping from one place to another to reach the princess's room. I knew her end was very near and for a reason, I was there. Inside the room, the lights were put off but due to the full moon, a kind of dim light was present. The princess was unaware. I went near her and whispered in her ear, "The moon is full today and the beautiful princess is sleeping. She is dreaming about the forthcoming time in the kingdom. The whole responsibility is on the shoulders of the princess herself. To serve all the purposes, the princess needs to have powers and most importantly, she needs to live for the people of her kingdom. A shepherd lives in a hut, nearby the palace and he has brought a small gift for the princess but he fears to reveal the gift before the princess for he doesn't know whether his gift will be accepted or not. But he knows surely that the gift is for the prosperity of this kingdom and if there is ever a need of his life then he will not step back from giving that." Just after, I completed the line, the princess (Although she was sleeping) put her hand on my mouth and said, "Don't say that, I'll not let him die for me." And before she could have finished her sentence, she woke up. She feared for a moment but she was not clear still about whether the incident was true or dream. She asked me, "Am I dreaming? And if not, what are you doing here?" I replied, "Princess, It's not a dream. It's true. I already told you the reason when you were sleeping." The princess again asked, "But that was the dream and I saw you just now." I said, "Well, that was an art, which was taught to me by my father. I can enter anybody's dream. By the way, we do not have enough time; I have something to show you."

The princess, "Yes, you were talking about some responsibility, what's that?" But before I could have answered her question, I had to eat the fruit also after one bite by the princess herself. I knew if I revealed the truth she'll never eat the fruit. Rather I said, "Oh, I am feeling hungry, do you have something for me to eat?" She said, "Yes," and offered some fruits to me, which were already there in the room. But I refused those fruits saying those are tasteless. Then I revealed the fruit, which was with me. I asked her- "Have you ever heard about this fruit? This is not found in this kingdom, it's found rarely in the jungle. It's the sweetest fruit and I am going to eat it. But you are the princess, how can I eat it before you? I must offer it to you before I will eat it." The princess laughed and said, "No, you can have it for you are hungry. You can bring the same fruit for me tomorrow, I can wait." I replied, "But I have respect for the royal family and so for you, if I'll take this fruit before you taste it then it'll be your insult and I'll never forgive myself for that crime." Now before she could have said anything, I said, "Please Princess, have a bite of this fruit and let me put off the fire of hunger inside my stomach." She laughed and accepted the fruit, took a bite of that and returned back to me saying, "It's really sweet, I wanted to have it fully, but you are hungry, you need it more. I'll wait for tomorrow to have the same fruit."

"But tomorrow never comes, that's why I let you bite this fruit once," I said and started to eat the fruit.

Scene- Seventh

Perhaps, the script was written like that. Yes, I was attracted towards her beauty, but more than that, I was very much impressed with her innocence, naturalism and her great understanding level. I didn't know what love was? But I used to feel her presence whether I was awake or asleep. That night was going to be the last night of my life but I was not worried for I had done my part. The fruit was very sweet and it started to show its effect as I finished it about half. I felt like all the energy of my body getting converge towards my heart, but I was not feeling any pain in that process. I felt very tired but managed somehow to stand because there were certain things which were necessary to share with the princess. At the same time, the princess was getting quite better moment by moment. I understood that the bane was getting transferred upon me. After a moment I was about to fall but the princess supported me and asked, what happened to me? I asked for a glass of water. Also, I warned her, not to inform anyone. She ran and brought the water very soon. I was laid down on the floor. She was looking quite worried to see my situation and also there were a lot of questions in her eyes. She made me drink water, put my head in her lap and sat there itself. Then she whispered in my ear, "What has happened to you and why are you not letting me call for any help?" I laughed and said, "No purpose will be served by calling anyone. But I have a wish, will you fulfil it?" She said, "Say it soon." I told her the story of my father about the unfairness that happened with him by the cruel king and asked her to take revenge from the king by defeating him. I also asked her about the temple which was situated across the river and suggested her to visit the temple, whenever she feels lack of power. And I said to her that this kingdom needs you very much; Take care of you and of your people. And I stopped for I did not have the energy anymore, even to say a single word. I was just looking in her eyes. I prayed to God to give me a little energy just enough to say three more words and my wish were fulfilled. I said to her, "You are beautiful."

Scene- Eighth

I saw then, she kissed my forehead, but I was no more there. I wish I were there. She sat there like a statue. At dawn, people rushed in the room. All the formalities were done. My father was informed. Needless to say, what his situation was, he remained silent for weeks. Yes, he had started work again from the very next day. He would go to the jungle with the sheep daily. One day, the princess went across the river to visit the temple. The priest was already present there. She offered her prayer to God and while she was returning, the priest came to her and said, "You can't go without knowing the truth, your purpose is not served yet." The princess replied, "What do you want to say? The priest made her understand each and everything in detail, also how did I take the effect of the bane upon me from her. She kept on hearing the whole story.

At last she said, "How can somebody love me that much?" She started crying, "You, the shepherd, you cheated with me.

You didn't let me know about your love. You just lived your love. You didn't give me a single chance to show my love." I said, "I love you, Princess." But she couldn't hear it. I wish she could have heard. She didn't stop and kept on complaining- "You did very wrong, after all, who had given you the right to save my life? I wish I could have understood the situation that night. You played your role very nicely and now it's my turn. I promise you to take revenge from the cruel king but wherever you are, please promise me that you'll be mine and only mine in our next birth." She fell down saying this. And I said, "I promise."

She was a brave girl. She gathered the armies from every possible source, planned the way, she was going to fight with the cruel king. Her forefathers were great warriors, so was she. All happened in a pre-planned manner, and she got the victory. That day, she cried a lot. She went to my old home, tried to feel my existence there. That day, I was ready to do anything to hug her. I prayed to god and went near to her. The art to enter anyone's dream was still known to me. I was just waiting for her to sleep. She went inside the home; nobody lived there at that time. She sat nearby on a chair, put her head on the table and slept for a while. I was waiting for the moment and whispered in her ears, "Dear princess, I am happy. I am here to say thanks to you. Today, you have played your role. Now I can plan my travel from this place. But at last, I want to hug you once." Suddenly a thunder rumbled; she stood up and hugged me. She could feel me for a moment only, and then I lost my existence.

Scene- Last

I stopped then, for I didn't know what happened after that. A beautiful girl stood up among the people who were listening to my story. She said, "I know what happened with her, can I tell further?" She was present there from the very beginning, but I didn't notice her because I was so lost in the story." I was eagerly waiting for listening to the girl. She started to say, "The news of her victory spread out like fire, many kings and princes approached to marry her, but she didn't even talk to any of them. She had decided to remain unmarried throughout her life. She went to the priest again one day and asked about when will she meet the shepherd?" The priest told her about this place and said, "In your next birth, you have to come here and one day, a person will come here and will tell the story of this birth, then you will understand the boy is nobody but the shepherd himself."

She continued saying, "She handed over her kingdom to her commander and lived as an ordinary citizen up to some years. She passed away when she was about 40 years old. Once, the priest had said to her that in the next birth, she will meet her love at the end of the first decade of the twenty-first century in India, near the temples of *Khajuraho*."

One of the people asked her, "But how do you know it all, and how did you remember it all?"

She just said, "Because Love can travel, even beyond the births". All started clapping then, as she began to move gradually towards me. Yes, she was the princess. I recognize her looking at the way, she was stepping forward, with her curly hair, and her beauty was natural. I couldn't believe at the moment that she was in front of me. But she was there. We couldn't say anything more. We just hugged each other but were unable to stop the water, coming from our eyes. Those moments were so perfect. We were just watching each other. After some time, people again started clapping. Then a cute boy appeared there from the mob and asked, "What are the names of you both in this birth?" We just laughed to hear the question because we were also unknown to each other's name so far. She replied, "Rani." Then the boy looked at me and expected an answer. I smiled and said- "Mohan."

Moral- "Love can travel, even beyond the births."

Mohan in Village

Although Mohan was studying in a town area, he belonged to a beautiful village and the village was one of the smallest villages of Madhya Pradesh state. The village was situated amidst a jungle. Up to the radius of five kilo metres, there was nothing except the jungle and the property of jungle, that is, Trees, a small river and animals etc. There was not even a road. Buses would leave passengers of the village, five kilo metres far from the village. From there, people used to travel on bullock cart via *pagdandi*.

When Mohan was about 10 years old. After appearing in examinations of 6th standard, as usual, he went to his village in summer vacations.

Mohan's uncle loved him a lot, during those days, he purchased a bike Bajaj M80 model. It was also the only bike available among the nearby villages. Mohan used to call him *uncleji*. So in the summer vacations, Mohan was very happy, especially to meet his grandparents and his cousin brother *Rinku bhaiya*. Mohan with his elder cousin brother used to make several plans to visit the places nearby the village and used to play different indoor and outdoor games. Mohan used to feel like he was in heaven there.

Rinku bhaiya was matured enough to get the permission of riding on the bike. They used to visit nearby places on the bike. Especially the jungle and the dam, which was being constructed there on the river. They used to sit on the mud rocks and would discuss many matters related to mysteries.

They also imagined many characters formed by the clouds and created stories around those characters. Sometime he would say, pointing towards clouds that the cloud having the shape of a demon, is a demon in real. He is coming towards the earth at a very high speed. He is trying to come on the earth from years but since he is very far from our earth, it's taking time, but soon within one year he will reach the earth. He has a sharp-edged weapon with him. He is coming to destroy the earth or to rule on the people of the earth. He will kill the person, whoever will oppose his decision.

Rinku Bhaiya- "So Mohan! I have made enough arrangements to save my life, have you done anything?" After listening to such types of stories, Mohan would get scared and ask his grandfather about the truth of the cloud-shaped demon. His grandfather would laugh on this matter and would tell Mohan that he need not fear anymore because there is nothing like that, *Rinku* was just joking with him. Mohan smiled and became happy.

Part-II

Mohan enjoyed his life at the village at its full pace, though he was not aware of it. We often value the things which are either far from us or which we have lost. Yes, this is one of the biggest truths, which is generally ignored.

Once Mohan had attended a function of a classical dancer who was Padmshri and Padmbhushan awarded. After the program, it was announced, if anyone is interested in asking a question related to her artistic life. Mohan just stood up and asked: "Mam,

How are you so good in this art of dancing and how can I be like you?" The Lady smiled and replied, "God has been so kind to me and this art is his gift. I am practicing dancing since my childhood and even at the age of 52, today I practice it to improve myself. It's never enough. When I practice it, I forget everything else and get lost in the dance, and as far as your being like me is concerned, you already have stepped in that way. Your willingness to be like that, just get lost in whatever you are doing and something original will happen, something pure will happen. You won't be able to recognize it at the time, but on the day of the result you will understand it by its fragrance, people will hold you on their shoulders, I think you got your answer, didn't you?" Mohan was silent for a while, but luckily just another moment he sensed the situation and replied: "Yes Mam, thank you."

So Mohan enjoyed his life because he was so lost in the lifestyle of the village that he didn't even know about his whereabouts. He would sometimes go with the cows and buffaloes and would try to find that where they go? Having a lot of doubts in his mind, he would go to his grandfather and would ask, "How is it possible that you just leave the cows and buffaloes free at dawn and in the evening they come back on their own to their respective owners. Do they too have a memory like us?" His grandfather would smile for a while and would make Mohan understand with satisfactory answers. Up to the age of five years, which Mohan spent at the village, his grandparents were everything to him. He didn't even talk to his father during five years of village life. All his purposes were being served very nicely with his grandparents only.

And the day came; when Mohan was asked to leave the village to start his study, rather say he was forced to do so. He cried so much but nothing worked. Even his grandparents couldn't stop him. He was carried to a town, which was a totally new place for him. His parents used to live in a rented house in the town. His father worked in the electricity board and his mother was a teacher. Mohan was asked to rest for a week and then he will be admitted in a reputed school of the town on 1st July 1990. The week passed so quickly, while Mohan was crying, making a senseless attempt to return back to the village. But unfortunately, nothing worked. Besides, 1st July came so fast. The task of Mohan's admission was assigned to his *uncleji.* This was going to be his 1st day in the school. In the village he often used to visit the school in his village for his mother was a teacher there. But that was just like a playground for Mohan. No attendance, no homework, no force to go to school, what else does one want to be happy?

But there, in the town, the things were different. So officially this day was his first day in the school. The formalities were going on; amid the conversation between the teacher and his *uncle ji* he was asked his date of birth. Mohan was astonished for nobody asked this question to him before. He was asked again, "What's your birthday, dear Mohan?" Mohan was silent again for he didn't know the answer. To celebrate birthdays was not the culture of his village; even every day was like his birthday there. The question was then shifted to his *uncleji.* He was also silent for he too didn't know the answer. But just another moment his *uncle ji* replied, "1st July Mam! He was born on 1st July 1986." Perhaps he knew what the date of that day was? Yes, that was 1st July 1990.

"Congratulations, Mohan! Your admission is confirmed in standard 1st."His teacher congratulated Mohan. Mohan was still staring her very strangely so far. She again asked, "So Mohan, when will you start attending the classes?"

"From today itself Mam," His *uncle ji* replied and he left Mohan in the school for the whole day. The very moment Mohan started crying very loudly but the teacher caught him very fast and with her smiling face told *uncle ji* that don't worry it happens. We shall take care of Mohan from now on, you can come back here by 4:30 PM to receive Mohan. His *uncle ji* left then.

And as soon as his *uncle ji* left him, the drama started at its full pace. Mohan cried like never before. All the teachers tried their best to make calm him but nothing worked. For the 1st time, he was present among weird people, weird environment and weird students, while crying; all were appearing like aliens for him because nobody was responding to his emotions. Nobody was there to listen to him.

Very soon, the matter was brought into the knowledge of the school in-charge. She was also a female. She entered the hall, where Mohan's drama was going on, everybody wished her, and all were silent. She asked Mohan to stand up on a stool in order to make convenient eye contact with him. Once she ordered Mohan to be silent, but Mohan didn't. Just another moment she slapped Mohan with full force, for some moments Mohan stopped. And after that, he cried even louder. That day even the *brahmastra* failed.

Eventually, she accepted her defeat and declared nobody can handle Mohan. She ordered her peon to go with Mohan and return only after leaving him to his home. Now that was something which she did in Mohan's favor. Mohan left with the peon to go home. That's how; it was his transient period from village to town.

The Love Letter

Mohan is a nine-year-old boy, a student of standard- 4 in a reputed school of the town. He lives with his parents in a rented house. He is fond of watching television, especially movies. His landlord has a television set. So sometimes, in holidays, he used to watch daily soaps and movies on the television. He used to watch the love scenes between a hero and heroine very interestingly. The dialogues between them, the style of heroes, every way the heroes acts and what not? He used to imagine himself at the place of the hero. He would weep when the hero and heroine got separated and would blame the situation. He would pray for the hero for his betterment. It can be said that he used to live in the movies.

One day he made a wish to search and meet his heroine, and after some moments, his wish was fulfilled. In his class, a beautiful girl, Rani got admission. Mohan decided to make her, his heroine. So he started to gather information about her, from every possible source. Fortunately, Rani lived nearby his place. They used to come to school on the same trip as the rickshaw. He would listen to her every conversation with her friends to know more about her. Once he came to know that rani is a daughter of the police inspector of the town, but Mohan didn't let that fact affect him... He had decided that he will face every obstacle between him and Rani. Now he was trying to search the ways to talk to her, to sit just beside rani or even in front of rani in the rickshaw, mostly he used to make the place in accord to his convenience.

He was a sincere boy in the class and at home also. He used to complete his homework and prepare the notes in the time. Most of the students used to carry his notes to home for reference. But now the preference was rani. No doubt Mohan had chosen her as his heroine, but to complete the story like a movie, it was equally important to build his image as a hero to her. Mohan decided to become more sincere. He would complete his homework before time and would offer his notes to rani. In the class, during the test, if Rani were unable to answer any question, then Mohan would write the answer on a piece of paper and pass that to rani so that rani could answer that and save herself from punishment. Mohan used to feel very happy by helping rani in such ways. By default, Mohan was becoming more intelligent day by day; his performance improved dynamically. His teachers were surprised but were unable to know the reason behind it.

Rani was an average student. Mohan used to help her in her studies. If due to some reason, like-illness, rani was unable to come to school, Mohan would go to her home and asked about rani's health from her mother; he even offered his notes to her mother for rani. For an excuse, he would say, "Tomorrow, in our class, the notes will be checked, and students will be punished, if they have not completed, my home is just nearby, so I thought I should help your daughter." Rani's mother would smile for his innocence and offer him some tea, but Mohan refused that, saying "I am in a hurry, another time." Thinking that, taking tea will not leave a good impression on rani's mother and would leave for home with a smiling face.

Another day, Mohan went to her home without informing, he saw rani, enjoying with her family. He just stopped and hid behind bamboo trees, that were in front of the Rani's home. Now and then he was looking at rani. Rani saw him, but because rani's family was present there, she couldn't call him. Mohan waved his hand, rani saw it and smiled. But there was something, Mohan was not happy with. Actually, rani was talking to a boy, seated beside her. Mohan was getting possessive; he left the place feeling unhappy. Next day, on meeting her, he asked rani about the boy she was talking to yesterday Rani told him that he was her brother. Mohan replied "Then, it's okay." Rani asked again, "Why, what happened?" Mohan said with a smiling face, "No, nothing."

Mohan's friends and other boys were also attracted towards rani; they used to gossip about rani and her beauty. Mohan didn't like that and made them aware that rani is a daughter of a police inspector of the town. It's dangerous to gossip about her in this way. But when they asked in return, "Then, why do you talk with her?" Mohan replied, "Because unfortunately, she is my classmate and I am bound to help her otherwise she may complain about me to her father, so dear friends whatever I do, it's out of fear." And Mohan was getting a little bit more serious about rani. Many a time, he found himself dreaming up different scenarios and how would he respond. Like- if his enemies (the bad boys of his class, who gossips about Rani) kidnap Rani, then he will save her and become a hero in Rani's mind.

At the other end, some of Mohan's classmates didn't like the friendship between him and rani. Though Mohan had justified himself, after all, they were getting closer and his classmates didn't like that. One day one of them asked Mohan, "Do you love Rani?" Mohan got scared after hearing this for the first time, he thought, what will happen, if by somehow my father comes to know about it? So he refused the matter immediately by saying "No."

Part-II

In this universe, every creature is bound by its own limitations. Sometimes people feel suffocated and limited like there's nothing they can do. There are moments they feel like a puppet while someone else is pulling strings. Mohan felt a sudden pause in his story as if it was time for Mohan's rivals to act up and ruin his story... One of Mohan's class fellows put in a lot of effort to know about the truth of his story. It was Neeraj, he asked Mohan, "Nowadays, you don't take an interest in anything except Rani, tell me the truth, as much as I know you, I am sure that you love Rani." Mohan sensed something wrong but as our senses have their own limitations, he reacted according to the pre-decided script.

Mohan's heart was beating faster and faster. He said, "Yes." But in return of sharing the secret with Neeraj, he took a promise from Neeraj that the secret will not be revealed before anyone else. Now it was time for next the step to be taken.

Neeraj said, "Mohan, why don't you tell Rani that you love her?"

Mohan replied, "So far, the feelings are one-sided, she considers me only as a friend. I don't know if she feels something for me in her heart or not?"

Neeraj asked again, "Okay, tell me what do you two generally talk about??"

Mohan replied, "Never on this matter. we have only talked about studies so far".

Neeraj asked, "When you smile at her, does she smile back?"

Although Neeraj knew it already because he sat just behind Mohan but he wanted it to hear it from Mohan.

Mohan replied, "Yes, she does, but what does it mean? Every smile cannot be proof of love, she smiles just like that."

Neeraj said, "Oh no Mohan, if a girl smiles, that means she loves you and that's it."

Now Mohan was sure that Rani loved him just as he does.

Neeraj said, "I have an idea. I will tell you how you can share your feelings with her."

Mohan suspected a foul play and said, "Now don't tell me that I should propose her directly. No, I can't do that because his father is a police inspector and he can lock me up in jail."

Neeraj answered, "No, it's not like that, you don't need to say it out loud to her and your purpose will be served."

Mohan asked eagerly, "Okay, then tell me."

Neeraj said, "Write a love letter and give that to her."

Mohan suddenly replied, "That is way riskier, suppose if somehow her father comes to know about the letter, what then?"

Neeraj said, "It's not possible, after all, she loves you too and in the matter of love the boy needs to be courageous enough to take the first step."

The next day Mohan planned to write a love letter. It was not a difficult task for him because often, he used to write answers on pieces of paper and pass it to Rani. Just this time, he had to express his love instead of an answer to a question. Suddenly he took a piece of paper and wrote, "You are my darling and my *jaan*."

He looked at Neeraj, Neeraj said, "Don't delay it. Pass it to her."

Mohan tried to get Rani's attention towards him by winking his eyes and with a cute smile. Mohan folded the piece of paper and threw it towards Rani.

And this was the historical task, done by Mohan in his life so far. That changed his life in a way. The task turned out to be a turning point in Mohan' life. Because he was studying in a kind of school, where there were many boundaries drawn for the students. Of-course they were for student's betterment but at that time, students don't understand that. Mohan had broken a rule. In an environment, where even thinking about a love letter, is considered a serious crime. And it's enough as a reason to expel him from the school. Mohan was thinking about the possible punishments he might have to suffer from.

At the other end, Rani was not surprised at first, because she used to take many pieces of paper from Mohan as written answers to prevent her from punishment. But this time why did Mohan throw that when there was no question needed to be answered? She thought while unfolding the piece of paper.

Here Mohan's heart was beating very fast as if it was about to burst out of his chest. But he was just sitting like a statue awaiting the response to his confession.

Eventually, Rani read it, she opened her mouth in wonder. It was a love letter, she had never imagined something like this can happen with her. Suddenly she looked at Mohan, Mohan tried his best to show that he was busy with some another work, as if he knows nothing about the letter. As girls can't keep anything to themselves, Rani was trying to draw the attention of at least the students nearby her. Mamta was her friend; she turned towards Rani and asked her, "What happened? What are you reading? What's written on the piece of paper and why you are so serious?" While firing questions at Rani, Mamta was getting serious too, as if something dangerous had happened with Rani. She took the paper from Rani's hand, read that and asked her, "Who gave it to you?" Rani pointed at Mohan. Suddenly Mamta asked Rani to complain about it to the teacher, who was present in the class at the moment. Rani was unable to understand anything and was in a dilemma about what to do? Mamta turned the issue into a bigger one, Rani had to take some action and what could she do? She went to the teacher and handed the letter over to the teacher. She was saying something to the teacher and during the conversation, Rani pointed out at Mohan once and sat back at her seat. Mohan was witnessing everything silently.

Part-III

Mrs. Gupta was the teacher in the class. She called Mohan, all the students drew their attention towards Mohan. Mrs. Gupta asked Mohan, "What's written here?" Mohan was silent but when Madam asked another time, Mohan read the letter as it is before all students of the class, "You are my darling and my *jaan*." The whole class was silent for some moments; even madam was staring at Mohan who was standing so still. Because Mohan had done something, which wasn't expected out of any student in the school. Mrs. Gupta slapped Mohan with a very high force and that action broke the silence in the class. Everyone in the class was murmuring about the incident. Mrs. Gupta called the peon and handed the letter over to the peon and asked him to go to the Principal's office with Mohan to and show him the letter. Peon took the letter and went with Mohan to the principal's office. The peon said to Mohan, "Stay here until I come back," entered the office.

Mohan had never imagined that the story could take such a turn and land him in front of the Principal's office. He was a little scared. Mohan thought "Because the matter is with the principal now and he can take any action, including my expulsion from the school. Oh god, why did you have to make Rani so beautiful? Her beauty made me express my feelings in a love letter to her. But I'm sorry, it's not your mistake. Perhaps I went wrong somewhere. I know that I spent five initial years of my life with my grandparents in my village. Though the village was surrounded in a jungle, I was happy there. They loved me so much. And one day my parents brought me to this town to turn me into a civilian so that I could turn their dreams into reality. I know that my mother and father are putting in their best efforts to make me reach the heights I dream of. They definitely won't be happy with this incident. Now perhaps they will send me back to the village, but this time I won't be happy there because I would have failed my parent's dreams. Oh dear parents, I'm sorry. I know that I won't be able to face you after the crime I've committed. Oh dear mother, I wish to get just one more chance so that I can positively prove myself. Today I've done something wrong that has not been done by anybody in the history of this school. If I get an opportunity, I will put my every effort to fulfil your dreams and I will get something positive out of it. Something no student in the history of the school has achieved and I will try to dilute the effect of my negative image."

Then he thought about his grandfather, whom he loves most and as if he was present there to help him.

Mohan asked, "I've made a mistake, now how should I answer the principal."

And he remembered one of the lessons' he had learned from his grandfather.

"Mistakes are like some impurity mixed in a glass of water, now if you mix anything extra in the glass to hide the impurity, the dirtier it will look. But every time you can minimize its effect by accepting your mistake in a way and of-course by mixing the pure water in it".

After some time the peon was outside the principal's office. He asked Mohan to go inside the office; *saheb* is calling you inside and he left the place. But Mohan had prepared himself enough to face the principal *saheb* by being simply as he was.

Mohan entered in the room.

Mohan requested, "May I come in sir?"

The principal said, "Yes, come in," and ordered Mohan to sit on a chair, which was just in front of him. Silently, Mohan took the place. The principal drew his full attention towards Mohan. Looking at Mohan's eyes, Principal sir, "You are Mohan, studying in the fourth standard."

Mohan- "Yes, sir."

Principal sir-"So you have written it".

Moan- "Yes, sir."

Principal sir- "What's the name of the girl?"

Mohan-"Rani."

Principal sir- "So, you have written this letter to Rani, why?"

(Mohan was silent for a while)

Principal sir- "Tell me, why?"

Mohan- "Sir, because…"

Principal sir- "Because you love her, Do you?"

(Mohan again remained silent)

Principal sir- "Tell me, Do you?"

Mohan- "Yes, sir."

(Principal sir was shocked for a while after hearing "Yes" as this was the first case of its kind in the school, but he didn't show it because he had to handle the situation in a way and he was a master of handling such situations, the remaining conversation proves that.)

Principal sir- "Mohan, what do you know about love?"

(Perhaps he was interested to know about the roots of the incident.)

Mohan- "Sir, I am such a small boy, what can I know about love? But whatever I have understood so far and heard about love, I will tell you."

From the very beginning of my life in the village, my grandparents used to take care of me. They love me a lot, and I love them too and will love them forever. Then my parents brought me to this town, they wanted to see me on the heights, they see their future in me, they also love me and I love them too and will love them forever. Today, because of Rani, I study more and I love her just like I love my parents and grandparents. I also love you, the teachers and the school, because you all are helping me to fulfil my parent's dreams.

Principal sir- "Whatever you understand about love, that's not wrong. But the way you expressed your love, that's not suitable for the environment of the school. See Mohan, to love someone is not a crime, but to do something like this at a wrong time is a crime. You come here to study, so pay your attention only to your studies. As I understood you, you also would not like to involve in such things that can stop you from fulfilling your parent's dreams. At least you should learn to control these emotions within you. Okay, tell me one thing. Have your parents or grandparents ever gave you a love letter saying they love you or have you written a love letter to them?"

Mohan- "No, sir."

Principal- "Does it mean that they don't love you?"

Mohan- "No sir, they love me and I love them but we understand it, there is no need to express it in written form."

Principal- "Exactly Mohan, love is an emotion that doesn't need any written form. That can only be felt. So can I expect from you that you will not express such emotion in any undesirable way?"

Mohan- "Yes, sir."

Principal sir- "And you will pay your attention to your study only?"

Mohan- "Yes sir, now on you won't get any complaints about me."

Principal- "Okay, you can go now."

Mohan- "Thank you, sir."

(He got out from the office with a happy face and went back to the class.)

Mrs. Gupta called Mohan and asked what principal sir told him. Mohan replied that the principal sir has asked him not to repeat it again. Then Mrs. Gupta said to Mohan, "Okay, go back to your seat." Mohan sat back there and opened the book.

Part-IV

Today, Mohan didn't choose the rickshaw to go home, he went alone. Because somehow he had faced the teacher and most importantly the principal, but he didn't want to face his fellows in the rickshaw. "They will definitely turn the case into a big issue among them to chat and to make fun of me," Mohan thought. A lot of thoughts were coming to his mind; like- Rani might complain about the letter at home and his father, the police inspector would arrest him and put him in jail. "I wish, Rani doesn't do anything like this to put me in trouble. After all, I have helped her in many ways. As I guess, she will not do anything like this, but what if somebody else approach him; I wish, nobody dares to," he thought.

At home, Mohan didn't talk to anybody. He was just responding in yes or no. Same-day in the evening, somebody knocked on the door. Mohan opened the door and Rani's father was there. Mohan was shocked for a moment. But then Rani's father asked about Mohan's father. Mohan replied, "No, my father is not at home right now. He has not returned from his office yet."

Rani's father said, "Okay" and left. Now Mohan thought that how would he survive in jail? His father returned home from the office but asked nothing. Mohan also wanted the same. Two days passed. Then Mohan felt somewhat lighter than before and told his father that the police inspector was asking about him. His father replied, "Oh yes, actually he had some important work in my office, so he might have come here to seek me for some help. Anyway, his purpose has been served."

Mohan's father- "Why, what happened?"

Mohan- "No, nothing. I was just informing you."

Mohan heard a lot of gossip about himself from his fellows in the rickshaw, in the classroom, at the playground and where not. But Mohan was busy to dilute the matter by studying hard. Rani didn't come to school for two months. One day just before the exams, Rani came to school to collect the admit card. In the class, the teacher asked Rani about her being absent for so long time. Rani was silent, but the teacher sensed the situation and stared at Mohan with anger in her eyes. The teacher told Mohan, "You are responsible for this girl's absence." Mohan was also silent. Then the teacher asked Rani, "Did your family come to know about the letter?" Rani said, "Yes". The teacher again asked, "Who told them?" Rani replied, "I did."

Exams were over. Mohan was an average student so far, but he was expecting a better result this time to serve his purpose. He had worked hard to get the desired result after all. The day had come. That day, the principal sir himself was announcing the result of each class. "Now comes the turn of standard four and the first position goes to Mr. Mohan." Principal Sir said. And everyone was shocked for a moment. Even the principal sir confirmed it by seeing the name of topper another time but history was written. Principal Sir congratulated Mohan. Everybody was clapping for Mohan. Mohan's eyes were searching for Rani but she had not come to collect the result that day. Mohan enquired about her and found that his father had been transferred to another place. He just wanted to see her once, but she was not present.

That day, while returning home, he was thinking, "I was just provoked by movies but if the result of all this is the first position in the class then perhaps I did not do anything wrong." Mohan came back home with a smiling face that day.

Mohan in love

Mohan felt very happy after receiving a mail from the HR department of Wipro Technologies Limited. He was selected in Wipro during campus drive. The mail was about his joining date. He had to report at the company office on 27th July 2007 at Hyderabad. And most importantly, he was supposed to go with his medical checkup, at least 15 days before the joining date. The HR manager had also sent him a list of affiliated hospitals with the mail.

Mohan called his friends, who were going to join the same company and asked them if they had gone for the medical checkup. He also called some seniors who were working in the same company and collected some important information from them regarding the medical checkup. From the list of hospitals, he chose a hospital, which was situated at Pune. Because his cousin brother, Arun was in Pune. Arun was working as an engineer in a software company. He decided to stay with him in Pune for two days for the medical checkup.

Mohan also talked to his cousin brother, Arun and gathered some information about the train that would be convenient to reach Pune. Arun asked Mohan to carry some particulars for him from Bhopal. Arun's family was in Bhopal, so Mohan happily agreed.

Mohan reached Bhopal a day before he was supposed to get on the train to Pune. He took Vishakha aunty's blessings by touching her feet. Vishakha aunty was Arun's mother. They discussed on some family matters. Then she asked suddenly,

"Mohan, do you know Sofiya?" Mohan remained silent for some time because the combination of the two subjects "Pune" and "Sophia" was happening again. Yes, he had listened to the two names seven years ago in connection with each other. He went into flashback.

It was at his cousin sister's marriage where he saw a beautiful girl, Sophia, for the first time. At first, he couldn't believe his eyes. It felt like a dream. He pinched himself and wondered, how can someone be so beautiful? He was a worshiper of art and beauty. And his encounters with such art and beauty always left him baffled and acting weird for some reasons. In his head, Mohan titled Sophia as 'The most beautiful girl on earth.' Mohan was serving water to everyone. He went near Sophia and offered her water. She took the glass in her beautiful hands and thanked him. Mohan's elder brothers were staring at him, thinking why they didn't think of this idea. They called Mohan over and asked him to take care of some errands out of the house.

Mohan was just fifteen years old at that time. He asked his sisters about Sophia and got to know that she is from the groom's side of the family and lives in Pune itself. The next day marriage ceremony ended with '*Vidaisamaroh.*' Sofia also left with the bride and her baraat. He wanted to meet her again and was eagerly looking for opportunities. He prayed to God to make them meet and if nothing else, at least let them be friends.

A year later, half of his wish was fulfilled. He went to Pune again to his cousin sister's home for a birthday celebration. That's when he met Sofia again. During his two days in Pune, he tried to talk to her, but it didn't work. They played cards together in a group. Sofia even served food to Mohan. But Mohan was afraid, and it was holding him back. Instead of his failure at friendship with Sofia, he enjoyed his two days in Pune. Just because he got to share the same space as the most beautiful girl on earth.

Mohan is twenty-two years old now. He had gone through many ups and downs from that time to the present when he was planning to go for his medical checkup at Pune. He might have forgotten many things related to him, but he didn't ever forget the memorable moment of hearing a sweet "Thanks" from the most beautiful girl on the earth.

Next moment, he heard, "Mohan, do you know Sofiya?"

"Yes, yes, I know her. She is a good girl, a very beautiful girl," he replied.

Part-II

The conversation started.

Vishakha Aunty- "Actually the family basically belongs to our area itself, but they had shifted to Pune a long time ago."

Mohan- "They?"

Vishakha Aunty- "Sophia's family."

Mohan- "Hmmm…"

I knew that.

Vishakha Aunty- "They have sent the proposal for marriage, of their daughter Sophia with…"

Mohan – "With?"

Vishakha Aunty (with smiling face) – "With Arun."

Mohan- "Oh, wow what a relationship that would be."

Vishakha Aunty- "Hmmm... How is she at household duties, and do you know about her qualification?"

Mohan- "As far as the household duties are concerned, she is perfect in that. Because when I was at her home once, I saw her taking care of everything. She is really a very nice girl and deserves a bond with Arun Bhaiya."

Vishakha Aunty- "And what about her qualification? Your brother wants a well-qualified girl. She should be a science graduate at least, and I support him too at this point."

Mohan- "Hmmm… Me too. But I don't know about her qualification. Actually, I rarely talked to her."

Vishakha Aunty- "No problem, you are going Pune. You can ask about her qualification. I believe that you will judge her correctly about behaviour etc. I shall give you the *Patrika* and a photo of Arun that you can handover to her parents. They asked me to send these things."

Mohan- "Okay, Aunty."

A person can't hold all the beauty, that is scattered in this world. Mohan considers Sophia as the most beautiful girl on earth. All of his dreams related to Sophia were breaking. He somehow managed himself to remain physically active during the above conversation with Vishakha aunty, but his heart was not accepting the truth. So far, he was dreaming about in a one-sided relationship with Sophia, that could have turned into something, but The Almighty had written something else.

Next day, he left Bhopal for Pune and reached there next afternoon. Arun was already there to receive him. Arun had reached there after taking special permission from his boss for an hour. Arun called a cab for Mohan. He gave him the address of his flat, handed over the keys of the flat to him and left for his office again. Mohan reached the place in one hour and ten minutes. Meanwhile, he acted as if he was not new in the city in front of the driver. When Arun returned to the flat in the evening, Mohan didn't talk to him much just a few whats and hows. But he didn't forget to phone Vishakha Aunty, and at his home about to inform about his safe arrival and that he is about to go for his medical checkup the next morning. He also inquired about the way to reach the hospital from Arun's friends.

Next morning, he reached the hospital at the right time, went through his medical checkup timely and left for Sophia's residence. But he didn't know the address of her home. So he called up the number which Sophia's uncle had given him once. Sophia's another uncle, who lived at Pune itself, picked up the call and explained him the way. Mohan was surprised at how easily things were going. Later he came to know that they all knew about it. They knew he was coming to Pune and the very purpose. The address, which Mohan was given, was of the shop owned by the uncle himself. He welcomed Mohan and phoned at Sophia's home. He told them that Mohan didn't have the address of their house, so he made him stay at his shop itself. He offered a cup of tea to Mohan and discussed general things with him. While Mohan's heart was beating a little faster because there was a possibility to meet someone special very soon. And after some minutes, a beautiful girl appeared in the shop. Yes, she was Sophia.

Mohan didn't believe it at first. After all, he was seeing Sophia after such a long time but because of the presence of her uncle there, he acted like he was ignoring Sophia and was still interested in uncle himself. While Sophia was saying thanks to her uncle for helping Mohan find the address as Mohan was new to Pune. It might have been difficult for him to find the address. All this while, Mohan was just watching her silently, how she was presenting herself. "Nothing changed in her; she is still the same Sophia he had met years ago," Mohan thought. They left the shop for Sophia's home. The home was just a five minutes distance from the shop. While walking, they didn't talk much apart from the general matters like- where was Mohan staying in Pune, why did he come here and the most touchy question of the conversation was that "Oh really, you remember me? Mohan answered all the questions one by one, and at last, he smiled and answered the touchy question as, "There are some people in the world, who can't be forgotten because they secure their place in your heart forever in just a few moments." Sophia just smiled after hearing that line and next moment they arrived at the home.

Part-III

After so many years he was meeting Sophia and only for some hours, on the presence of her family. Mohan was unable to read Sophia's mind. But he started dreaming of a future with Sophia. There was no clear idea about where he would get his posting place by the company, although Pune was one of the options, the final decision depended on the HR. Next day he was supposed to board the train to back to Bhopal and then his hometown. And so far it was only Mohan who was feeling all this. Sophia was just behaving naturally. Then Mohan remembered what he had wished for. He just wanted Sophia in his life even if it was as a friend. Perhaps because she was the most beautiful girl on the earth. But that moment he forgot something very important, that could change the words of his wish a little bit. And that was the purpose of his coming to that home.

"Oh my God, what I was thinking about! I have come here to watch Sophia's behavior and to know about for her qualification so that I can tell it all to Vishakha aunty and Arun Bhaiya can marry Sophia," Mohan thought. So he had to amend what he had wished for. From "At least as a friend" to "Only as a friend". He could never forget what Vishakha aunty and Arun bhaiya had done for him. He remembered when he had come to Bhopal to prepare for competitive exams PET and AIEEE. Vishakha aunty had allowed Mohan to stay at her home for some days until he was able to find a room for him. Arun bhaiya used to drop Mohan daily to his coaching classes and pick up from the institute too. Thinking of all that, Mohan just took out the Patrika and Photo of Arun Bhaiya; and handed that over that to Sophia's mother. Sophia's mother also asked a lot of questions regarding Arun Bhaiya and his family background. Mohan answered each of those very calmly. Till the moment, he had accepted that Arun Bhaiya and Sophia were made for each other.

After the conversation, Mohan asked for permission from Sophia's parents to go back to Arun Bhaiya's flat, where he was staying. Because the next day he was supposed to return back to Bhopal on a train. He had already made a reservation for that. All family members, including Sophia, forced Mohan to stay that night there itself. And the plan was something like- next day; Sophia's father will drop Mohan to Arun Bhaiya's flat. Mohan agreed, and the next moment, they started gossiping in their folk language.

Now Mohan was in doubt and he thought, "Does Sophia also consider him as a friend or is she just responding to him because he is a far relative of her? Whatever the case is, I will try my best to impress her to be my friend." And for that purpose, he just had fifteen hours, in which six to seven hours will be spent while sleeping. Mohan was very loyal to Arun Bhaiya too. He had answered every question Sophia's parents had asked him about Arun Bhaiya in a positive manner.

He successfully bonded with each member of the family which included Sophia's two brothers; Ravi, Saagar and Sophia's parents, by his nice behavior. He discussed some interesting events of his hometown with Sophia's parents. That made them happy. They wanted to hear more stories from their hometown. Perhaps they were missing their hometown after listening to Mohan. Humans are so weird sometimes. Mostly, people settle in cities to earn a better standard of living. But whenever they visit their hometown for festivals or holidays, they don't forget to show their attitude. Or maybe their struggles in the city turn their hearts into stones. But still, they miss something inside them. They still want to breathe in the fresh and open-air, which is generally absent for most the citizens in a city. Their life becomes so hectic that one even doesn't have time to ask their family members that how are they? In cities, for most of them, life means just to earn and eat. They look just like robots.

Mohan thought that he won't be able to continue in an environment where there is no time to even breathe. He was getting worried thinking about the future when he will be doing a job here. Meanwhile, Sophia called him outside where she was sitting on the stairs with her mother. Mohan went there and sat next to her mother. Sophia was one stair up and was playing with her mother's hair. Then her mother again started asking some questions from Mohan about Arun Bhaiya's family. Mohan saw Sophia, typing a message on her cell phone. Mohan thought of a trick to have her number.

Mohan said- "Sophia! Whose phone is this? Is it your father's? At least it can't be yours. Am I right?"

Suddenly Sophia replied- "No, it's mine."

Mohan- "Then, what is its number? I am sure you don't know, and that will prove you don't own this gadget".

Sophia- "No, I said this is mine, its number is 9096******."

Mohan- "Oh, you are lying. Let me check."

He dialed the number on his cell phone and the bell rang at the other end.

Sophia (giggling) – "Now is it okay? That proved this is mine."

Mohan (smiled) – "Yes, you are right. It is yours."

"And the purpose is served." He thought.

Part-IV

Sophia was not a fool like she acted during the last conversation. She just helped Mohan get her number. Because of her mother's presence, that type of conversation was necessary to get her number. After all, they were part of a conservative society and asking her number directly might have left a bad impression. Mohan had to take care of that all too. And what if Sophia had refused to give her number? Mohan would not have accepted that ignorance. So it was a safe card from Mohan's point of view.

Her father returned home at 10:30 PM. They all took dinner then. Mohan also played the synthesiser, which was at a corner of the drawing-room in their house. He played just for a little while to show that he can play that. After all, he had someone to impress. Then he asked Sophia if she wants to play the synthesiser, but she refused saying that she doesn't know how to. And that was the truth. It was 12:00 midnight, and they preferred to sleep than carrying on with gossips.

Early morning, 7:00 AM they woke up. Sophia and her mother had already woken up earlier to perform household duties. They all took breakfast. So according to the plan, Mohan was to leave with her father for Arun Bhaiya's flat. They all took a promise from Mohan, to visit them again, whenever he comes to Pune city. Mohan assured them positively, waved his hand, saying bye to Sophia and her family, left for his next destination.

He came back to Bhopal by next day morning. There he explained everything positively about Sophia and her family to Vishakha aunty, as fine as possible. And returned to his hometown the same day. After reaching home, he felt happy and was eagerly waiting for 27th July' 2007, on which he was supposed to report at Company's headquarter at Hyderabad, for training purpose. He had reserved his ticket in Dakshin Express to go there. And the day came very soon. Finally, he had reached Secunderabad Railway station. He had gone there with his two friends Neeraj and Mayank. They reached the flat of one of their common friend Manish, who was residing in Hyderabad itself for he was already working there as a software engineer in an MNC. Manish and Mohan used to live in a common wing of a hostel, during the final year in college days. Even their rooms were in front of each other. The area was Madhapur, near High tech city of Hyderabad where Mohan's office was situated.

Mohan reported at the office on 27th July with his friends Mayank and Neeraj. Within one week, they searched their respective rooms and flats on rent. They were put in the same batch of thirty students, in which rest 27 trainees were Bengali. They mingled with the Bengali trainees very soon, because there was no option left. There were two departments, testing and coding. Mohan's batch belonged to coding. Now Mohan thought of giving some velocity to his story of the most beautiful girl on the earth. Because he had settled there and apart from the learning in the training period, he wanted to spare time for beautiful Sophia. He had her number but didn't know how he should start the conversation? Soon he got an idea when he watched a movie "*CASH*" with his Bengali friends. There was a joke in the movie, which was used by the hero to start the conversation with the heroine. Mohan typed that joke in his cell phone's create message field, pasted "Hi" in the last of that message and pressed the button to send to Sophia. He was eagerly waiting for the response from her side.

The joke was-

"Santa aur Banta ghode par jarahe the, santa aage aage, Banta peechhe peechhe. Santa ne Banta se peechhe mudkar poochha- Oye tera ghoda kidhar hai? Banta ne kaha- Ghode par hi to baitha hoon.

To Santa hanste huye bola- Poochhne me kya harz hai?"

"Santa and Banta were riding on horses. Santa was leading and Banta was following. Santa asked Banta- 'Where is your horse?' Banta replied- 'I'm sitting on the horse'. Santa said- what's the harm in asking?"

The same day in the evening he got a reply on his cell phone. Yes, it was Sophia.

"Hi Mohan, How are you? Have you joined the company? Sophia."

And this way, the conversation started again between them.

Part-V

The universe had played its role in bringing Mohan and Sophia together as friends. The gate was open. Now it was Mohan's duty to move further. So he replied generally to Sophia.

Mohan- "Yes, I am in Hyderabad right now and will be here till my training is completed. Then, there is a probability to get Pune city as a posting place."

Sophia- "Oh, wow! When are you coming to Pune?"

Mohan- "October last, but that would be confirmed after completion of training."

She was happy to know that probably, the posting place will be Pune. It meant that she was also willing to see Mohan in Pune again. Sophia sent an SMS to him.

"Life is a weird mystery.
?
?
?
?
It won't get solved just by pressing the keypad."

Mohan took this SMS as an invitation to friendship. It felt like Sophia was inviting him to open that door. Do something, take the initiative. Now you are doing a job, what else you are waiting for?

Mohan replied, "I extremely want to solve it, but don't know what really this life is."

Sophia replied, "Oh Mohan, don't be so serious, it was just an SMS."

This was a pure googley from Sophia's side. Mohan sent a good SMS about friendship to her and got a touchy reply.

Sophia- *"When you win, I will proudly tell the world, "Hey…! That's my friend", but when you lose, I will sit beside you, hold your hand and say "Hey...! I am your friend" Take care."*

No doubt, she had accepted Mohan's friendship. It got clear by the next SMS sent by her.

The SMS was titled "Friend Book" and was like a question paper, in which Mohan was supposed to fill the blanks. Mohan filled those blanks within seconds and sent it.

"Friend Book
Name- Mohan,
Age-22,
Birth Day- 1 July,
Pet name- Mannu.
Favourite food- Fried rice and homemade whatever. Favourite hero- Shahrukh.
Favourite heroine- Sridevi.
Favourite colour- Navy blue, Blood red.
Favourite song- there are many.
Favourite friend- Dileep, Mukesh.
Girl friend- No one."

Then Mohan demanded from Sophia, to fill the friend book for him too. And she filled it and sent on the same evening.

"Friend Book
Name- Sophia,
Age-21,
Birth Day- 8 March,
Pet name- Sophi.
Favourite food- Uttapam.
Favourite hero- John Abraham.
Favourite heroine- Aish.
Favourite colour- Black, Blue, Yellow and red.
Favourite song- All sad songs and many.
Favourite friend- Pihu, Kavita, Varsha.
Boy friend- No one."

Mohan also sent the acronym of Sophia to her.

"S-Simple,
O-Original,
P-Perfect,
H-Honest,
I-Innocent,
A-Artistic,

Do you know? These are the great qualities in my friend, who is reading SMS now."

"Go to the mirror, and you will see the best and lovely friend of mine. Just smile once, and you will see the world's most beautiful smile. Yes, that's my friend."

The SMS express was accelerating. There were some interesting SMS which made the relation of friendship deeper.

Sophia- "Music is the best way to express your views about a person, so tell me a song that comes in your mind when you think of me."

Mohan- "It's not a song that comes in my mind when I think of you. Rather it's you, who comes in my mind when I hear any song."

Sophia- "Well, if all songs are for me, then I am proud of myself."

Mohan- :-) Anyway the song is '*Mera dil bhi kitna paagal hai*' from the movie "*Saajan*". Now send a song tone.

Sophia- Nice song, Mohan! But no song comes in my mind when I think of you. Just joking, :-) the song is '*Bolna halke halke*' from the movie "*Jhoom baraabar jhoom.*"

And Mohan had not listened to the song even once. It was 11:30 PM, there were a handful of people roaming on the road nearby. Mohan called his friend Manish and enquired if he has the song in his collections. Manish said yes, and another moment Mohan was ready to go to his flat to listen to that song. The flat was a KM far from his place. He went there and listened to the song 4-5 times and returned in 1 and half of an hour. Now that was something crazy, but he did that just because he just wanted to.

Mohan had read in books and watched in movies several times about friendship and love but never had lived through those very feelings. After a certain time, he always used to think that now this is the time to propose her, but another SMS by her used to stop him and make him aware that there are some more steps in this path. What a collection of messages she had with her! Every new SMS by her used to tell that love is something even beyond it. Mohan was enjoying those feelings in full flow.

Mohan- "*Teacher- Attendance, please!!*

Chintu- Yes sir, Mintu- Yes sir, Golu- Yes sir, Punnu- Yes sir, Sophia-?? Sophia-?? Sophia- yes, yes, sir.

Teacher- what happened, are you thinking about Mohan? Good Morning."

Sophia- :-) Nice message, Good Morning, what are you doing?

Sophia- Oh, really! :-) How much do you miss me?

Mohan- A lot, can't describe it just in words, tell me one thing, do you miss me too?

Sophia- *"I will take a brick and write on that How much I miss you and then I will break it on your head to show you how much it pains when I miss you."*

Mohan got the message and was thanking God for these precious moments. Somebody in some corner of this world cares for him that much. That was just unbelievable. But that is what these relations are all about. The steps were not finished yet.

Part-VI

Each SMS used to be a new step on the path of their relationship. Every new SMS used to bring them closer and make the relationship deeper. They used to talk a lot over calls too. Sophia would disclose her secrets, her hobbies to him. Many times he thought and tried to propose her, but whenever he tried to say something, his lack of courage created a long awkward pause in the conversation. So far, he had only heard that it's a difficult task to propose someone, but during those days, he was living the difficulty. The scenario was more than enough to understand that Sophia and Mohan had become at least best friends of each other. They both understood it too. Whenever his Bengali friend Kalyan alias KP, used to encourage him to propose her, Mohan used to come up with a nice excuse. He would say- "these three words 'I love you' are very small to express the feelings I have for Sophia".

Once he called Sophia and said- “I want to say something to you.”

Sophia- “Yes, I am listening.”

Mohan- “Actually, I was saying that…that…”

Sophia- “Yes, say please.”

Mohan- “Oh, Sophia, you understand what I want to say, right?”

Sophia would smile and say- “No, I don’t.”

Mohan just would ask, “How are you” and all that. Then he would end the conversation with another unsuccessful attempt to propose her. By the way, the SMS express was running in full speed. She sent some more very touchy SMS to him.

Sophia- *Aapko bhool jana namunkin si baat hai, aapko na ho yakeen, ye aur baat hai. Jab tak rahe gisam, tab tak rahoge yaad, ye saans toot jaye, ye aur baat hai.*

Forgetting you is an impossible thing, you don’t believe it that’s another thing.

You’ll be in my memories as long as I draw breath,

If my breath leaves me that’s another thing.

Sophia- *Aaj socha ki SMS kya bhejoon? Aap muskuraye in, aisa paigam kya bhejoon? Koi phool to hamen maloom nahi, jo khud gulshan ho, use gulab kya bhejoon.*

What SMS should I send you I think, what should I write that you smile. I do not know the language of flowers, and anyhow what good will sending roses do, you're a bouquet in itself.

Sophia-*Kya kahe inke kuchh kaha nahi jaata, dard meetha hai par sahaa nahi jaata.*

Rishta ban gaya haikuchh is qadar aapse, ki bina baat kiye aapse rahaa nahi jaata.

How to say anything, I'm beyond speaking
This pain is pleasurable but beyond bearing,
I'm connected to you in such a way now,
Living without you is beyond thinking.

Sophia- "I trust you" is a better compliment than "I love you" because you may not always trust the person you love. But you can always love the person whom you trust.

Mohan- *Dil ki awaaz ko izhaar kahte hain, jhuki nigahon ko ikraar kahte hain. Sirf jataane ka naam ishq nahi hota, kisi ki yadon me jeene ko bhi pyar kahte hain.*

Giving voice to this heart's desire is my confession,
Lowering the eyes is your consent.
Expression of emotions isn't love in itself, living in and with your memories is also love.

Sophia- Make a heart which never breaks, make a smile which hurts, make a touch which never pains, make a love which never ends.

Mohan- *Nazron me hamaari koi bas gaya hai, hum kaise kahen ki wo tum ho. Hum jinke liye jamaane bhar se kar sakte hain bagaawat, tum hi bataao hum kaise kahe in, ki wo tum ho.*

There's someone I see everywhere she lives in my eyes it seems, how do I say it's you.

I can rebel against this whole damn world for that someone, tell me, my dear, how do I say it's you.

Sophia- *Jab kisi ke sapne kisi ke armaan ban jayen, jab kisi ki hansi kisi ki muskan ban jaye, bepanaah pyar kahte hain use, jab kisi ki saans kisi ki jaan ban jaye.*

When your dreams become someone else's ambitions,
When your smile becomes their reason for happiness
It's called unconditional love when your breath becomes their life.

Mohan- *A deep and great relation doesn't say that whenever you are in problem, I'll be there; it says that you will never be in a problem if I am there.*

Sophia- *Enemy+you= friend, Hate+you= Love, Tears+you= smile, Confusion +you= Solution. Nothing+ you= Everything. Me+you=....?? Send a nice answer.*

Mohan- *The whole night I thought about the equation that what should be the answer to Me+ you= ...? And I found that, it's Me+you= Life. Isn't it interesting? Let hope wear the wings. :-)*

He felt like flying even beyond the sky. The situation was absolutely indescribable. And one day, there were continuous bomb blasts in Hyderabad city. One after another, about eight more blasts happened at different places in the city. Mohan got the news just after reaching to his hostel, while he was taking evening tea. He watched about those blasts on television. Then he remembered that one of those blasts happened at the place, where he was coming from. Mohan thanked God for keeping him safe after the tragedy. Just next moment, some of his well-wishers called him to insure about his safety. He responded very calmly to all of them except Sophia's call. He exaggerated the situation to her.

He said- "Thank god, I am safe; otherwise, I would have died today. Do you know? I was just five minutes distance from the blast point."

Sophia also said- "Really, you must thank God, and have you informed at your home?"

Mohan replied- "Yes, my mother called me."

Sophia was so happy to know that Mohan was safe.

Thought of losing someone can be so unbearable sometimes. Nobody ever will want to lose his loved one. Sometimes the relationship becomes so deep that even on losing our loved one we never find ourselves ready to accept the very truth. Mohan never wanted to lose Sophia. He decided that day of not waiting anymore to propose her because who knows? Next bomb blast and game over!!

Part-VII

Mohan got the news that the marriage of *Arun Bhaiya* with Sophia was almost impossible for two reasons. One- their *kundali* didn't match. Two- there was an age gap of about seven years between them. Their families were satisfied with each other, and for this reason, they were ready to ignore the non-matching of their *kundali.* But the second reason, related to their age, was unacceptable to both. *Arun Bhaiya* had not even seen Sophia's photo. The truth was the second reason of age, but Sophia felt like she was rejected by *Arun Bhaiya* and his family. Sophia was very sad and shared her feelings with Mohan that evening.

It was not the first time when the process of her choosing a suitable groom was stopped in midst due to some reason of dowry, age factor or some else kind of dissatisfaction from either side. Sometimes the family from boy side would get agree for the relation just by watching her photo and would confirm the relation in another meeting when Sophia and the concerned boy used to see each other in the presence of all. But every time some kind of dissatisfaction would happen and that would become enough reason to stop the process. Sophia was used to it all and tired too. But this time there was someone to share this unfairness, happening with her. And that someone was Mohan. He showed his sympathy to her and made her understand that the pairs have been already made in heaven. He gave her some ray of hope by saying- "You will be paired very soon with a very worthy guy, enjoy your current home till then. Do you want to leave your home, your family, so soon?" And Sophia would laugh on hearing this statement. Mohan used to feel very happy about making Sophia smile at times. And this time he decided to give her something better to be happy about. Yes, he decided to propose her.

Sophia's parents were in a hurry to arrange her marriage, but they were not able to find the right guy because of their very busy schedule. But Sophia's marriage could take place at any time on fulfilling the requirements of their dream family. Mohan didn't want to become a loser at least from his side. He prepared himself very well on 14th October 2007. He called Sophia on the same evening, and said- "Sophia, I have to say something to you and that's very special to you and me."

Sophia- "I am listening."

Mohan- "Do you know, today is 14th October?"

Sophia- "Yes, so what? Is there anything special today?"

"Yes," Mohan replied.

"And what's so special today," She asked again.

Mohan- "Sophia…I…."

He paused for fifteen to twenty seconds.

Sophia broke the pause and asked- "Are you there? What were you saying?"

Mohan- "Sophia…"

He paused again for about 10 seconds. Then before breaking Sophia could break the pause, Mohan started speaking.

He said-"Sophia, I… I love you, Sophia".

And there was a pause of 2 minutes.

Mohan- "Sophia, are you there?"

Sophia- "Yes, I am here. My mother has come, I shall talk to you later."

Mohan- "Yes sure, I will wait, bye."

And the conversation ended.

Mohan was very happy that day after proposing a girl the first time in his life. He couldn't forget how afraid he was while he was confessing to Sophia. But eventually, he did it.

"I don't mind the outcome, at least I have confessed what I feel,"He thought. That evening, he got no SMS from her side. He felt he shouldn't have said anything to her.

"Perhaps she is comparing me with other guys. I should clarify my feeling by sending a heartfelt message, "He thought. And he sent his feelings in the form of SMS.

Mohan- "Sophia, this was not in my heart from the day, I had met you in Pune before three months, but this is a story, which started seven years ago. It started at the marriage ceremony of my cousin sister when I saw you there the first time."

Mohan- "I agree that you deserve a far better life partner than me, but whatever I feel for you, I told you. Sophia, it's your life, and you have every right to live it in your own way. Trust me, there is no wrong intension in my proposal. I just wanted to express my feelings, and I did that. To love someone is not a crime. You can't imagine how nervous I was, while I was confessing my love."

Mohan- “You had asked me what was on that day, 14th October. That day, I proposed someone special, someone, who understands me, someone original with no masks on her face.”

Up to three days, there was no reply in any form. No SMS, she didn’t even take his calls. Forth day Mohan called her again and she picked up.

Mohan- “What happened to you? Did I say something unexpected that day?”

Sophia smiled and said “Perhaps.”

Part-VIII

Their conversation continued-

Sophia- “I knew that there may be something like that in your mind, but I had not expected that in that way.”

Mohan- “Oh, you mean to say that I should have done that in a boat? Provided you don’t know swimming, and there would be no option left for you apart from saying, yes.”

Sophia- “No, I was saying that I was just shocked.”

Mohan- “So?”

Sophia- “So what?”

Mohan- “What is your answer?”

Sophia (After a pause of five seconds) - “I don’t know.”

Mohan- "Let me tell you that I won't get hurt if you say no. I just wanted to express my feelings for you, and now I am feeling lighter than before. I don't expect anything from you, but I shall try my best to fulfil your expectations. You know the reason. You have every right to choose a life partner of your choice. I shall pray to God for giving you a worthy life partner. May God always keep you happy with whomever, you marry. Perhaps you took it as a formal proposal like a boy does for a girl. In our case, it's just a coincident that you are a girl, and I am a boy. But in reality, the proposal was from a worshiper towards the beauty, towards the originality and towards the innocence. However, I consider you one of my best friends, with whom I can share my feelings. Which, I can't share with everyone. Cause you are special for me for a reason, you know."

Sophia- "I respect your feelings and very happy to know that someone thinks it all for me. Someone saw originality and innocence in me. Let me tell you that there is no question to say 'NO' to you. But saying 'YES' will be a lot from my side. You must understand that I am a girl. And saying yes or no is a very tough decision from a girl's point of view. Let me tell you that you are among the very few people in my life, whom I can trust. I, too, consider you, one of my best friends. I also don't expect anything from your side. I learnt a lot while talking to you; especially you helped me to build up a positive attitude in me. From your side, you have unloaded your feelings and feeling lighter, but I want to live those feelings up to a lifetime. I can't let you unload them. Feelings mean a lot for a girl. First time in my life, I got an opportunity to taste Love. I want to live each and every moment of it. I want to feel every part of Love. Let me not tell you what is inside me? Let me live it. Let me feel it."

And the conversation ended when Sophia's mother entered the room where she was in.

Mohan got a mail on his mailbox. And that was regarding his posing place because his training was just about to finish within the next week. He got Pune city as his posting place. Obviously, he was happy to read that on the mail. He informed his family, and then he called Sophia to inform that he will be reaching Pune on 1st November. Meanwhile, Sophia sent an SMS to him.

Sophia- *"I .... You. 1- Want. 2- Love. 3- Care for. 4- Need. 5- Hate. 6- Kill. 7- Help. 8- Trust. 9- Will be with. 10- Forget. 11- Like. Fill the correct answer for me, from the given options."*

Mohan- "All options are correct for you, just leaving the options fifth, sixth and tenth, now send it for me."

Sophia- *"I will kill you if you will ever try to forget me."*

And it took about seven years to pass those seven days, but finally, he was in Pune city. He stayed with his cousin brother Arun Bhaiya for about two to three days until he found a room for him nearby his office. He shared his happiness with Sophia. He was happy to be in the same city she was living in. Soon he started working on a project in his office. The schedule was very hectic, and he did not have any time to even talk to his family or Sophia during office hours. There in Pune, he met with Sophia at her home in the presence of all her family members. Also sometimes he used to meet her outside her home like in the market near her home or at a local railway station. But they hardly had any words to speak with each other. There used to be many pauses of several minutes on cell phones.

By the way, Sophia never answered. She was quite satisfied with the journey of love so far. Perhaps she feared that if she expresses her feelings in front of Mohan, then she may lose him; because doing so, might have turned Mohan, a little careless from his side. The feelings were very safe in her heart. They used to talk often, even till today and will carry on till their last breath. But they talk about nothing, about something, which is indescribable. Regardless of whom they marry, they promised each other to carry on the relationship till their last breath.

Mohan remembered his wish to become friends with the beautiful "Sophia." And the wish had been fulfilled.

First Date...

Either the desired or nothing. Either he would ask for his favorite dish, or he would prefer to be hungry. Either it should be National Institute of Technology to pursue B. Tech. Or he will prefer to drop a year and prepare to face the competitive exam again. Mohan was an adamant person since his childhood.

Eventually, he managed to get admission to National Institute of Technology. There he was a scholar of Electrical Engineering among 60 students, who had come from different corners of India; while 4-5 students were from other countries too. During his first year, he came across many experiences. He learnt a lot. Though he was a Hindi medium student up to 12th standard, he faced little difficulties to grasp the things, which were taught in the class. But his friend was supportive enough to help him in this regard. Mohan used to clear his technical and non-technical doubts from his friends. Especially his roommates Nitin and Anuj used to tell him the meaning of tough words in the English language. Meanwhile, he also learnt a lot of cuss words as fun by default.

One day for the first time, he understood that the word 'Date' has another meaning too apart from a specific point of time. And that was something like- to go outside with your girlfriend, to spend time with her, to take lunch or dinner, to watch a movie and many things whatever she doesn't have problem with. The idea to go on a date was not bad; instead, that was attractive enough to make Mohan think about it. But to go out on a date, he needed a girl. And in Mohan's case, she'd have to be someone special. Someone beautiful, with a sound personality and open mind. He asked himself where he can meet the one he is looking for? And he got an answer on the evening of the fresher party in his college.

That day, after 4-5 months, the first-year students were allowed to wear the casual clothes of their own choice. The students were very happy to wear jeans and t-shirts after a long time. Same rules were applied to girls; they used to wear simple formal salwar suits and were not allowed to wear jewelry. No need to say that all those rules were totally unofficial and were in existence from years. The seniors were helpful, especially while giving treats, paying fares in the city buses, suggesting which author's books should be referred. They just demanded respect for them and nothing else. However, there were some special ways to handle some students who didn't know how to respect. According to seniors- to know the casual way of action is necessary to survive in society. Aristotle says- "A man is a social animal". And if he wants any help from another person free of cost then at least he must show some respect to him.

First-year of engineering is considered to be the most memorable part of engineering life. And the moments become even more memorable if those days were spent in a hostel with a lot of friends. By the way, her name was Kratika.

Kratika was selected miss fresher of the year. She had performed a fantastic classical dance and got a worthy reward of being Miss Fresher. She was very beautiful and had a sound personality. Mohan thought of selecting her as the girl he would take on a date. But he was not sure whether she was open-minded or not. To know that he was supposed to talk to her. And he thought of congratulating her for becoming Miss Fresher. Many fellows were already in the queue to congratulate her and were shaking hands with her. He waited until she was alone. Then he went near to her and said- “Congratulation Kratika, your performance was really fantastic, I was shocked.”

Now here was something, which Kratika didn’t hear from anyone apart from congratulation. She also replied in the same manner with a smile- “Oh thanks, but why were you shocked?”

Mohan- “Because generally girls are of shy nature and you danced very enthusiastically, I was just impressed.”

She was so happy to hear that she did something which others can’t.

Kratika- “Hearty thanks, by the way, what’s your name?”

Mohan- “I am Mohan.”

While the conversation was going on, Mohan’s friend called him, and he left the place saying that he will meet her some other time. She also replied- “Yes, sure.”

While he inquired about her branch, place and all; coincidently he came to know that Kratika belongs to the same group in which Mohan belongs. But in the first year, boys were not allowed to visit the girl’s hostel; they were unknown to each other so far. “Thanks to the Fresher’s party which made me meet her, “Mohan thanked God. She was pursuing her degree in architecture. The department was just beside the Electrical department. Mohan thought of informing her that they belong to the same group.

Part-II

One day, he saw her near his department during lunch hour. He went to her and conversation started.

Mohan- "Hi Kratika, How are you?"

Kratika- "Oh hello Mohan, I am fine. How are you? I didn't see you after freshers.'

Mohan- "I am also fine, actually I was preparing for the mid-semester exams."

Kratika- "Oh, well, how were your exams?"

Mohan- "Exams were okay, but I can't say about the results. Anyway, what about your exams?

Kratika- "Mine were okay. They disclosed the marks for two subjects. I topped in my class."

Mohan- "Oh, congratulations! By the way, do you know that we belong to the same group?"

Kratika-"Yes, I know it already, but don't you think that our group is not that active?"

Mohan- "Correct, that's why I have a plan to go outside with all members of our group for a picnic or movie, will you agree?"

Kratika- "Yes, I shall be ready all the time."

Mohan- “So picnic or movie?”

Kratika- “Whatever, I have no problem at all.”

Everything was programmed there. From the first day visit to the semester break, the timetable was already prepared, and the things were processing according to the timetable. First semester examinations were over, and students were going to their homes on semester break. Mohan went too, but like all, he was also missing his friends at home. One month passed, and they were again in college for the second semester. One day he again saw Kratika nearby his department. But this time it was Kratika, who approached him. And the conversation started.

Kratika- “Hi, Mohan, How are you?”

Mohan- “Hello Kratika, I am fine. How are you and how were your vacations?”

Kratika- “I am also fine but vacations were just fine because I was getting bored at home.”

Mohan- “Actually the same thing happened with me too, only God knows about how I passed those days.”

Kratika- “So did you make any plan to go somewhere outside?”

Mohan (with a giggle) - “Oh sorry, not so far. But I had talked to almost everybody in our group, and they are ready for it any time, now we have to decide where to go?”

Kratika- “Ok so, plan for it and inform me, and please let me inform in advance so that the plan doesn’t clash with another one.”

Mohan- "Don't worry; I'll inform you a week before."

Kratika giggled and said, "Ok bye, see you then."

Mohan- "Bye Kratika."

Mohan and Kratika were not so close to be known as boyfriend and girlfriend. They were not even friends. They just knew each other incidentally. Off course Mohan himself created the incident. Mohan had started attending personality development classes in the second semester, and for this purpose, he had purchased a bike because the coaching institute was far. So, during their meeting somewhere in the college campus itself, Kratika asked for a treat, Mohan didn't refuse and said- "Anytime Kratika."

Kratika accused- "What anytime, you also promised to go outside with our group but that hasn't happened yet."

Mohan- "Oh, actually I have talked to all of them, but they all are not free at the same time."

Kratika- "So what? We can also go with the ones who are free."

Mohan- "Ok Kratika, this Sunday we will go for a movie, and I shall inform to all. Let see whether they will come or not. Otherwise, we will go with whoever shows up. "

Kratika smiled and said, "Ok done."

Mohan- "One more thing; you will be responsible for informing the girls of our group in your hostel, and I shall inform all the boys, see you on Sunday, bye till then."

Kratika- "Yes sure… Bye."

The next task for Mohan was to plan for a picnic or a movie. He talked to his friends who were in his group and planned for a movie. Now, which movie? It was to be decided later. But one thing was sure that they were going for a movie on Sunday. Later his friends refused to go because they had made their own plans to enjoy Sunday. He informed Kratika about the refusal by his friends, also asked about the response from Sonam, who was the only other girl in that group after Kratika and waited for her response.

Kratika said- "Same here, Sonam is also busy on Sunday, but I have no problem. I can come with you alone too."

Mohan- "Ok then, be ready on Sunday."

Kratika- "By the way, which movie we shall go watch?"

Mohan- "It will be decided on Sunday itself, based on the movies they are playing in the theatre that day. We'll choose one of them."

Kratika (with a smile) - "Okay."

Part-III

Sunday came very soon. Mohan called her on the cell phone and told her to be ready by 4:30 PM for the evening show at Jyoti talkies, which was at 5:30 PM.

He reached on his new bike, at the right time to girl's hostel, where Kratika was staying. At 4:30 PM, he called her to inform that he was waiting for her outside the hostel. She replied that she was coming in just five minutes. And those five minutes took about thirty minutes for her to get ready. So far, he had only heard about the very truth that girls take more time than any other mammal on this earth, but this time he experienced that, the first time in his life. By 5:00 PM, she came outside to secure a seat on Mohan's bike. They moved towards the talkies.

Kratika- "So which movie are we going to watch?"

Mohan- "I don't know the name, but it's a nice movie according to the public report, which is running in the talkies, where we're going."

Kratika sensed that Mohan is not happy because she took so much time to get ready. And they remained silent during the bike ride till they reached Jyoti talkies. While driving, Mohan stopped by the petrol pump. Generally, he used to get the petrol fill for twenty rupees or hardly fifty rupees, but that day he got petrol worth a hundred rupees.

They watched the poster, pasted over there. Well, it was Mithun Chakraborthy's movie.

Kratika- "It's looking like a C grade movie, and you said its review was good."

Mohan- "Yeah, actually it's a B grade movie; Mithun Chakraborthy just played a guest role in this movie."

Kratika said, "Ok."

Then Mohan bought two corner tickets, and they went to the balcony. Getting inside, they found that hardly five or six people were there to enjoy the movie. And they were five or six people in number including Mohan and Kratika.

Mohan was trying to concentrate on watching the movie, but Kratika was not in that mood. Instead of that, she was asking personal questions to him. In a very short period, she had asked many questions about his personal life, like- his favourite dish, favourite place to visit, favourite actor, actress, movies, hobbies, favourite sports and career plans etc. Mohan answered all the questions one by one, but he was unable to understand why was she showing so much interest in him? But he sensed it very soon.

Meanwhile, something else caught Mohan's attention. And this was nothing but some romantic scenes running on the screen.

Mohan- "Oh, this actress is looking so gorgeous, isn't she?"

Kratika- "Hmmm… She is."

Mohan- "By the way, I want to ask something from you. May I?"

Kratika- "Sure."

Mohan- "Weren't you afraid, coming to the movie alone with me?"

Kratika- “What’s there to fear about? And I am mature enough to understand who is reliable and who isn’t. With whom should I go outside and with whom I shouldn’t? But why did you ask me this?”

Mohan- “Actually, you are attractive and anyone can be flat on your beauty, so I think you should have thought enough before planning an outside visit.”

Just after listening that she was attractive, she giggled for a moment and answered, “OH thanks for praising me but let me tell you that you are the first guy, I have come outside with and I am already concerned about my security, by the way, I also would like to ask something from you.”

Mohan- “And what’s that?” Kratika was taking time to ask the question.

Mohan- “Don’t think so much, you can ask whatever there is in your mind.”

Kratika- “Do you have a girlfriend?”

Mohan laughed on this question for a while and then replied “No, I don’t. Actually, there are girls I talk to, but there isn’t anyone special, to call my girlfriend.”

Kratika asked a lot of questions to Mohan to know his perception. Like whether he believes in love marriage or not. What qualities he is looking for in his life partner etc.

Mohan- “As far as my marriage is concerned, that will definitely be an arranged marriage until unless love happens, because love is something unpredictable. I shall definitely prefer a girl of my caste, of my religion and of-course fulfilling all the requirements according to our rituals. But when love happens, there will be no rule. Because when, how and with whom will it happen? Nobody can tell."

Kratika- "Are you sure you will fall in love someday?"

Mohan- "I can't tell, nobody can tell. I can just tell you that my doors are open. I won't stop myself from falling in love." Kratika was just looking in Mohan's eyes during the conversation.

Kratika- "I want to ask one more thing from you?"

Mohan (with a smile) – "Please ask."

Kratika (slowly) - "I don't know, from where should I start?"

Mohan- "Oh, come on yaar, don't think that much, I have told you that you can ask me anything."

Kratika- "What was your purpose of coming with me to watch this movie?"

Mohan was answerless for some moments. Anybody would be. People behave answerless for some time only in two cases, when the answer is very complex and when there is no answer. Instead, the answer needs to be thought upon, just to satisfy the person in front. This time there was no answer.

Part-IV

"Kratika, I have no girlfriend. I have seen many girls, but you are incomparable. You have each and every quality, which I was seeking in a girl to make her my girlfriend. You are not only beautiful but intelligent as well. I am also impressed with your presentation skills and perception. If you were my to be my girlfriend, I would feel like the luckiest person in this world. But this is not too late, the opportunity itself knocked my doors to introduce you with me. Please Kratika, accept my friendship request and be my girlfriend." Actually, she was expecting something like this, but she was looking quite neutral when she heard the real words in place of the above ones.

Mohan replied without any delay- "It happened just because of your desire to come outside for a treat."

Kratika (with a smiling face) - "But why only me? You could have come with Sonam too."

Mohan- "Because it was only you who wanted the treat, I have no problem with Sonam. Instead, I told you to inform and bring her too, but you informed me that she will be busy on Sunday."

Kratika (In a very relaxed mood) - "Oh…. Thank god, I don't know about what was I thinking? Now I am really feeling very light."

Mohan- "Be relaxed, one doesn't need any special reason to come outside with a group member. It doesn't matter whether they have come as a couple."

Kratika- “And what will you answer to your friends, when they will ask your whereabouts of today evening?”

Mohan- “It’s simple; I was with Kratika and watching a movie. What’s weird in it?”

Kratika- “Actually, I was asking because people may think of us as a couple.”

Mohan- “Don’t care about it. You and I, both understand that we are friends and only friends, then why to worry? And what’s there to worry about people’s perception? Let them think whatever they want. And we are not the only couple in Bhopal, who have come outside to enjoy this movie; there are a lot in our college itself. So don’t worry.”

Now if Mohan asked why she came with him in that case? There is no need to explain it. It’s common sense.

Anyway, the movie was over now, and they came outside. It was 8:00 PM.

Kratika- “Thanks, Mohan, I really enjoyed.”

Mohan (while smiling) - “Oh, then tell me full or even brief story of the movie.”

Kratika giggled to hear this and said- “I know, even you can’t tell. Can you?”

And Mohan laughed this time. Kratika- “So, where should we move further?”

Mohan- "Our hostel, I can understand that there is a restriction to get back to your hostel by 8:30 PM. I am also feeling hungry, and it's time to take dinner at our respective hostels."

Kratika- "Oh, that's not an issue, I can manage my entry inside hostel till 10:00 PM; I think we should have dinner somewhere outside itself. And I'll pay for that."

Mohan agreed to have dinner outside. He got his bike from the parking lot and told Kartika that he won't let her pay the bill this time for she was the one who had asked for the treat. They went to one of the famous restaurants in Bhopal and had dinner. Kratika paid the bill.

Mohan- "I can't force a girl too much for doing something, be it the payment for the dinner."

It was 8:45 PM, they started for their hostels. Kratika put her hand on his shoulder, this time. He dropped her at her hostel. Kratika thanked him with a cute smile. Mohan thanked her too, for coming with her. Mohan returned to his hostel then and just smiled.

He never went out with any other girl after that day, never waited for any girl outside the girl's hostel. He just wanted to go for a date, and the wish had already been fulfilled.

Via Allahabad Junction

During *Pune* times, Mohan had applied for the post of an officer in the Indian Air force. The written test for the same was conducted in *Pune* itself. Mohan managed to clear the first round of written test. Then he was called for an interview for the second round. For the purpose, he had to be present before the service selection board, *Varanasi.*

During July 2008 when he got the official call letter for an interview by the recruitment board, he was staying in Bhopal. He searched on the internet for the best possible train to reach *Allahabad* and found that there is only one train available. Also that it would take approximately 24 hours to finish the journey. Mohan decided that he won't go by this route; instead of that, he would catch a train from *Itarsi* junction. Only he had to manage to reach *Itarsi,* which is 2 hours from Bhopal. By this way, he could reach *Varanasi* within 16 hours, via *Allahabad.* So from the list, he chose *Mahanagri* Express.

The current status was not confirmed yet. On railways' site, when he enquired about the current status by inputting the PNR number, it was WL-4 by the time. "Oh God, I wish at least four people change their mind of travelling and cancel their tickets so that I can at least go by sitting on the berth if I get the status RAC," Mohan wished.

On the day of his journey, he put all the necessary documents and clothes inside a briefcase. The journey started when he reached Bhopal railway station. He searched the screen for the trains, which were to depart for *Itarsi.* He took a ticket of the general compartment to travel from Bhopal to *Itarsi.* Within two and half hour, he was in *Itarsi.* The train *Mahanagri* express was running half of an hour late that day. Mohan waited there itself and checked the latest status meanwhile. That was WL-2. “Oh shit!! Only two people didn’t cancel their ticket, but now nothing can be done because the chart is already prepared,” He murmured.

The train arrived at approx. 14:30 PM, he hurried to enter the train because he had to request some people if they would allow him to sit with them because the status of his ticket was on the waiting list. He did so and was able to secure a place to sit and put his briefcase beneath his seat. The train started moving slowly-slowly and in this way, the journey from Bhopal via *Itarsi, Allahabad* to *Varanasi* started.

He was cautious about his briefcase and was checking its presence beneath his seat from time to time. Approx. 2 hours before *Allahabad,* a person, who was sleeping on side upper berth in the same compartment, came down and sat on the lower berth among the people. When even after 15 minutes, he was not willing to go back to sleep on his place, Mohan requested him to allow himself to rest on his seat till the time he doesn’t go back there. The person said, “Yes” so Mohan climbed up to rest on the upper berth. Up to *Allahabad,* the person didn’t ask Mohan to vacate his seat, But Mohan himself came down two times and asked the person if he wanted to sleep now on his upper berth. Meanwhile, he checked his briefcase both the time. Yes, it was there.

The train reached at *Allahabad* by 01:00 AM another day, the train was supposed to stop there for half of an hour. Mohan watched from the top at his briefcase that was beneath the seat, where he was seated before going to the upper berth. Yes, it was still there. And after another two minutes when he checked again, his briefcase was not there. "What? It's impossible, let me check it by going down," He thought with a lot of tension. The briefcase was not there, he searched beneath every seat in that particular compartment because it might be possible that his luggage got misplaced after people had taken their luggage from there. And the briefcase was still not found. His worry mounted and Mohan asked people in the compartment if any of them had seen his briefcase. The people searched with him and found nothing.

Part-II

Some people inside the compartment suggested him to report to the GRP people very soon. "They can help you in this regard, because if somebody has stolen your briefcase, then the thief would not have gone very far from here," A person said. Mohan ran towards the GRP office, he met two policemen nearby. He explained the situation to them in the shortest possible time. They came with Mohan to the compartment and searched again for the briefcase, but found nothing. They suggested Mohan report to the GRP office very soon and see, what was the best possible solution.

Mohan ran towards the GRP office, he explained the situation again before the police in- charge there. "Sir, please do something fast, the train is about to leave in 10 minutes. I must reach *Varanasi* by early morning on or before 7:30 AM with the documents in the briefcase; the briefcase contains all my documents, which I have earned throughout my life till today," Mohan pleaded. "What was there inside the briefcase?"

The police officer asked. "Sir, Mark sheets of High school and higher secondary, all the eight semester's degree mark sheets, provisional degree certificate, character certificate, Passport, the white dress which I am required to wear before The SSB (Service Selection Board)during recruitment process along with the call letter from the Air force officials to attend the recruitment process." Mohan replied.

"Are you sure that there was nothing else in the briefcase? I mean, was there any money or expensive items like something, in that?" The policeman asked. "Sir, I am sure about what I have said," Mohan replied. "Then the briefcase was of no worth for the thief, he might have thrown it after checking it. So don't waste your time, go fast and search your briefcase near this place and also at both sides of this railway station, it might be possible that you will find it and there would be no necessity of writing the report," the police officer suggested to Mohan.

Mohan ran towards the exit gate of the railway station, went outside and tried to search his briefcase nearby there but didn't find it. He returned to go to another side of the railway station. In the midst, while going to the other side, he stopped for some moments, where the train *Mahanagri* express was boarded. He ran for the last point of the platform, reached there and found that there was nobody nearby the place up to 100 meters from the place. He was going through some of the very strange moments of his life so far. He felt as if the blood circulation had stopped in his body, he was not able to listen to anything going around him, he thought of his mother then. He dialed the number on his cell phone to talk to his mother. It was 1:25 AM midnight. One by one, he explained everything to his mother and went silent. From the other side his mother said, "Mohan!! Don't lose your control, firstly search on the other side of the railway station too, it might be possible that you would find the briefcase there and then go to *Varanasi,* explain the whole situation before the air force officials there, they may give you another date for interview and don't forget to take the holy bath in the River *Ganga,* also do visit the *Kashi Vishvanath* temple there." Mohan said, "Okay," and disconnected the phone.

Mohan made some unsuccessful attempts to find his briefcase here and there. But found nothing, he again ran towards the GRP office to write the report. "Sir, I have searched at every possible place, now it's 1:30 AM and my train is just about to leave, please do write my report so that I can show the official proof of losing the documents before the air force officials at *Varanasi,*" Mohan pleaded again. "Listen, if you want the report then forget the train, the process will take some time. We can't write your report before any proof, now wait here itself, I am coming after taking tea," The police officer said. Mohan had no option. He saw his train leaving *Allahabad* for *Varanasi.*

Part-III

Mohan was waiting at the railway station. He was able to see that the police officer was standing at the Tea stall, outside the railway station since the last half of an hour. It was 2:00 AM. The police officer came to Mohan and said, "You should get your report written at *Varanasi* Railway station, since you are going there itself and I don't want any such report to be written, when I am on duty, because doing so will prove that there was theft committed when I was active during my duty time. It will raise questions on my duty. But don't worry, my duty time will end till 6:30 AM, so after 6:30 AM you can get your report written because then there will be another in-charge." Without wasting a single moment more, Mohan returned from there and boarded another train, which was to leave *Allahabad* at 3:00 AM for *Varanasi.*

Mohan confirmed from some passengers about the timing, when this train would reach *Varanasi*. And he slept on one of the berths there because now he did not have any item with him to take care of. Apart from his wallet which was kept in his pocket, the clothes on his body and his body itself. After some time, he felt a little force on his body. He understood that the train had started moving towards Varanasi.

At 7:00 AM, Mohan reached *Varanasi.* There he went to the scheduled place, where he was supposed to be. All the candidates were showing their call letters to the air force officer who was present there to receive all of them and taking place inside the bus, which was there to carry the students to the air force station. Mohan approached the air force officer and explained his situation about not having call letter and all. The officer checked his name in his record and said, "Yes, your name is here on the list. But without the call letter, we can't allow you to enter the bus. You can reach the air force station by your own arrangement and explain your case before the officers there and let's see what happens."

"Sir, I have my driving license which can prove that I am the same person of the name, which is in your list, so please allow me to enter the bus," Mohan requested.
Officer asked to Mohan, "Do you have any proof that your documents were stolen. I mean, do you have the police report of that case?"

"Sir, they didn't write my report about losing the documents. I don't know why but they were not ready to help me," Mohan answered.

The officer refused to take Mohan inside the bus and they left Mohan there. Mohan was looking at the bus, which was going to leave him in front of his eyes.

Soon after the moment, he approached a person, having tricycle rickshaw and asked him, "How much will you take to drop me to the air force station?"

"Ten rupees," The rickshaw driver replied. "Ten rupees!! But it is too much, how far is the air force station ?" Mohan asked.

The rickshaw driver (yawning) - it's 6 km from here.

Mohan- No, it's only 3 km and I have been informed by the air force officer himself. So I will give you five rupees.

The rickshaw driver- It's because they travel this distance on their bikes or even on cars. They never realise how much it pains while paddling on the sloppy road. I won't take a single paisa less than six rupees and that's final. Come on, sit.
Mohan was also in a hurry; he sat on the seat and moved towards the air force station.
He reached there and reported at the gate of the air force station. There he was asked about the purpose he came for and he explained all that had happened to him. He got a pass from there and was asked to report at the central room where all the candidates were present. He mingled with them and enjoyed some tea and biscuits. Then an officer came thereafter ten minutes and announced about the program of that day.

The first program was document verification and they all were supposed to do it one by one, just after a rest of ten minutes from that moment. Mohan didn't wait for that time and went to the officer's room.

Part-IV

He reached the first floor and met with five-six officers, gossiping there, sitting on nice chairs around a circular table. They all started looking at him and one of them asked him about his purpose of being there. Mohan explained the whole story again in front of them.

One officer- "So what do you want from us?"

Mohan- "Sir, I had scanned all the documents and saved those in my mailbox. I can show all of those to you if you are have an internet facility here and I have my driving license still with me, which is proof of my identity. My name is there in the list of called students, you can check that. That would be proof that I had the call letter with me."

Mohan showed them his driving license; one of them saw that and matched the name with the list which they had with them.

The second officer- "It's okay that you are one of the candidates we called today for various tests. But how can we believe your story? Police or bank officials may have seized your documents, you might have committed some crime or you were unable to pay any loan."

The third officer- "Okay, do you have any proof regarding your documents getting stolen? I mean, have you informed the police? If yes, then can you show us the police report, saying the documents were stolen last night?"

Mohan- "The Police Officer in charge didn't write my report. He was not any help, even when I pleaded many times before him. He gave so many excuses for not writing the report. But I can try it at the *Varanasi* GRP office and come back here within half an hour with the copy of the police report."

Forth officer- "It will take time, we can't wait for you to come back here till then. We are just about to start the recruitment process. But don't worry; we shall give you another call letter, according to that you will be able to attend the recruitment process on next Sunday. You can come to us on that day with photocopies of the documents, police report about the stolen original documents and photocopy of the application which you will be presenting before your concerned higher secondary board and university to get the duplicate copies of the documents."

Mohan- Thank you, Sir.

Mohan took the call letter from them and went towards River *Ganga*. As he had nothing with him, he bought a towel and one pouch of coconut oil. Somehow he managed to take a bath in the holy river, dried himself with the help of the towel, wore the same clothes again and moved towards *Kashi Vishvanath* Temple. There was a lot of rush in the temple, after some time he engaged himself in a queue. After some time, he was inside the main temple, there he saw and touched "The *Shivlinga*". He prayed for blessings for self and wished for the betterment of his family, also spoke some lines which he generally uses to speak before the almighty.

"Sarvebhavantusukhinah, sarvesantuniramyah,
Sarvebhadranipashyantu, ma kashchiddukhbhagbhavet."
"Tvamewmata cha pitaatwamev,
twamevbandhushchshakhaatwamev,
Twamevvidyadravidamtwamev, twamevsarvam mam dev dev."

He was one of the true believers in the prayers. He felt a little bit lighter after coming outside the temple. He felt as if - he had sent a message to the almighty, now it was their turn to guide him. He went to the railway station then and bought a ticket of the general compartment from *Varanasi* to *Bhopal,* came back to *Bhopal* within 16 hours.

After coming to *Bhopal,* he applied to the Board office and at the university, to get the duplicate copies of his certificates. Within two weeks, he got all those, which were equally valuable like the original ones. After that, whenever Mohan looked at the word "DUPLICATE" written on the mark sheets, he thought of the incident, which was enough for accelerating his heartbeat. But eventually, he had gone through a tough experience.

Via Mumbai....

"Hello, May I talk to Mr. Mohan?"

"Yes, speaking."

"Sir, you had applied for the post of Project Engineer in our company, CDOT ALCATEL; you are shortlisted for an interview, which is scheduled to be held on 9th January at our Head Quarter in Chennai; By the way, where are you right now?" The lady asked.

"Right now, I am working for Wipro Technologies Ltd. Pune and residing here itself," Mohan replied.

"So, can you come to Chennai from Pune to attend the interview?" She asked again.

"Yes Madam, I'll be there on the right time at the mentioned venue," Mohan replied. She thanked and disconnected the phone.

On the 10th of January, there was a written test of a PSU company in Mumbai. So in order to attend both, his presence was required at both the places. On 9th in Chennai and on 10th in Mumbai, two different corners of India. Mohan planned his journey and booked the tickets accordingly. He downloaded the maps of Mumbai and Chennai, which was a new city for him and packed with all the necessary documents which were needed at the interview venue.

On 8th January the journey started after his departure from the guest house, where he was staying. He reached to Rahul's

Cineplex, which was near Pune railway station and booked a ticket for the next movie. The movie was "MITHYA," starring Ranbeer Shaourey, Neha Dhoopiya and directed by Rajat Kapoor. He enjoyed that and rushed to the railway station where a passenger train "Pandharpur Express", was expected to arrive within some minutes.

The train arrived at 00:30 AM, which was midnight. He managed to secure a seat on the train and by 4:45 AM, he was at *Dadar* station of Mumbai. He knew it from Mumbai's which station would be convenient to reach the international airport in Mumbai. The airport was at the nearest distance either from *Santacruz* station or from *Ville parle* station of the Mumbai local. But the stations were not on the route of the train; Mohan came from, just sometime before. So Mohan was waiting for a local train so that he could reach either of the nearest stations from the airport. He was waiting eagerly because he was going to travel by air for the first time. The local train was expected to arrive at 6:00 AM and arrived at the right time. Within 5 to 10 minutes he reached V*ille parle* station. About which he had discussed with some people on the train and came to know that *Ville parle* would be the best one in order to reach the airport. At 6:10 AM he rushed to find a taxi in order to reach the airport. On the train he also came to know that to catch the airbus, he should be there at the airport at least 1 hour before.

The flight was at 7:00 AM. So far, he was thinking that he is running about 50 minutes fast with the planned schedule. But now he was 10 minutes late from the desired time. Meanwhile, he was thinking this all and was on the way to the airport by taxi. He reached there at 6:20 AM. He entered quickly and got into the queue, after crossing that people were being checked by a machine. But Mohan noticed that he was missing something, he was looking at pieces of paper which were looked like lottery tickets and were held by almost every person, who was in the queue. Mohan asked about the paper to a person, who was just next in that queue and came to know that the piece of paper is nothing but the boarding pass of the flight, without which one can't even enter in the airbus.

"And from where can I get my boarding pass, so far I just have this computerized ticket given by an agent," Mohan asked.

"Go quickly to the respective counter of the company," The person replied.

The company name was "Go Air."

Soon he went there and asked for his boarding pass.

"Sir, Could you please show me your identity proof?" The lady at the reception asked. Mohan showed his driving license, collected his boarding pass and ran to stand in the queue. The queue was so long and it was 6:35 AM already. Then an officer of Airport authority came and announced, "If there is any person, whose flight is at 7:00 AM, can come by the shorter queue so that the one could be checked in earlier." Mohan ran towards the officer and showed his boarding pass. The officer helped Mohan and showed him the way to security. Mohan passed through the security and moved further.

There were many gates, where passengers were in a queue again. "But which gate am I supposed to go to? "Mohan asked himself. Then he saw that there was a number written above each of the gates. He searched everywhere on his boarding pass if the numbers written above the gates were matching with either number written on his boarding pass, and one matched. He thanked God and rushed to the gate. He showed his boarding pass to the security, which was on the gate and moved out. It was a very large ground and a bus was there as if the authority on the bus was waiting for someone. A person from the "Go Air Authority" checked Mohan's boarding pass and asked him to sit in the bus. Mohan took a seat and the bus left the place to catch the plane.

So far, Mohan had seen a plane in pictures and movies. But that day one of his dreams was going to come true. That was the last bus, carrying the passengers for the flight. Because as soon as Mohan and the remaining people of the bus, entered the plane, one of the air hostesses closed the door. It meant nobody will enter now on. They were beautiful ladies and perhaps that's why everybody was paying so much attention to them, when they were announcing the respective guidelines. Then the cabin crew came at the midst and explained practically, how to tie the seat belts. That time the air hostesses were copying all the actions of the cabin crew, standing at the front and behind respectively. Obviously, many were looking either at the front or at the behind.

Now it was 7:00 AM, the plane started to move. Mohan was at window seat; from there he saw many planes that were standing outside, while the plane was accelerating. The speed was getting faster and faster by the second. At the moment, he felt like the outside scenery is being tilted. And another moment, he was in the air.

Part-II

He remembered his days in the village, where he had seen aero planes a thousand times, passing above his village that is situated near about 12 kilometers from an international airport ***Khajuraho.*** *Villagers used to call them "Cheelgaadi". He used to wish to travel on those planes but he never imagined that his wish will be fulfilled with situations like the present one.*

And that day, the wish was being fulfilled; he was in the air, flying even above the clouds which he had wished to touch so many times. "If this plane had landed right here on these clouds, I would have walked here," Mohan thought and laughed upon his stupid thought. The cabin crew came with the air hostess to serve some light food and drinks, obviously on payments because the class, on which he was travelling, was an economic one. He bought a sandwich and a fruit juice.

The plane landed at Hyderabad airport after 1 hour. Some more passengers joined them at the airport and the plane flew again on its way to Chennai after a short break of 10 minutes there. The plane reached Chennai airport in just another 1 hour. At approx. 9:00 AM, Mohan was at Chennai airport. He came outside the airport and searched for an auto-rickshaw in order to reach the desired place where his interview was scheduled.

It was the south-east area of India, famous for its hotness. One of the auto-rickshaws drivers came there and asked Mohan where did he want to go?

"*Kottivakkam*, that is near to old *Mahabalipuram road*; I want to go there," Mohan replied.

The driver nodded his head in yes and asked Mohan to sit inside the auto-rickshaw. Mohan queried about the fare before sitting inside the rickshaw. "600 rupees," the driver replied. Mohan stopped himself from sitting inside. "What? 600 rupees!!! do you know I can go back to Mumbai on paying 600 rupees by train." Mohan stopped himself from arguing with the driver anymore. Because it was not the train, by which he came to Chennai; it was something else that is called an aero plane. And for that reason, Mohan had to pay a lot more than the genuine fare. Everyone, who comes outside from an airport, is considered a rich person, at least for an auto-rickshaw driver. By the way, Mohan started to bargain. Now the next difficulty was the language. The driver was talking in Tamil and Mohan was talking in *hindi*, repeating the whole in English too, hoping that the driver would understand either language. "*Kottivakkam*" and the amount of money were two words that were common and being understood by both of them. Finally, both were ready at 400 rupees. Mohan sat inside the rickshaw and went to *Kottivakkam*.

Mohan switched on his cell phone and took out the map of Chennai to match with the tower name on the cell phone screen with the map. He reached the destination within 40 minutes. He was hungry so, he searched for some restaurant. He bought some *samosas*, some *pani-pouch* and fed himself. Without any delay, He reached the destination, where the interview was scheduled. Mohan used the company's bathroom to get fresh and changed his clothes there itself. Mohan attended the interview. There were three rounds, one was HR interview and the other two interviews were technical ones. Mohan faced all of them and was told that the result will be declared within one month.

Mohan came outside the company office and searched for an auto-rickshaw to go back to the airport. This time he paid only 150 rupees because he didn't disclose that he was going to the airport. Instead, he told him about a place just nearby the airport. He reached there by 4:00 PM. The flight was at 9:00 PM. Till then, he waited outside the airport. At 7:00 PM, he entered the airport and went through the checking process. This time he went by the first bus to the plane. By 11:00 PM he was in Mumbai. He searched some guest house and hotels to rest and pass the night because next morning he was to appear for a written test of a well-known PSU, which was to be held at Guru Nanak College of Arts & Science, Guru TegBahadur Nagar, Mumbai. But no one allowed Mohan to enter inside the hotels for no reason. Perhaps that was night and he might be a terrorist, who knows?

Up to one and half of an hour, he searched but every effort was in vain. It was 00:30 AM. He caught a local train and went to the Mumbai CST. At the railway station, he laid down some newspapers to prepare a bed for him. He used his bag as a pillow and a shawl to cover himself. He rested there for the night. A cold morning in Mumbai, a hotter day in Chennai, again cold night in Mumbai, this all happened within the same day. A journey inside an aero plane and sleeping on newspapers at a railway station, this also happened on the same day.

Mohan woke up at 5:00 AM, prepared and got fresh at the railway station. He caught a local train at 6:00 AM and reached GTB Nagar, where the test center was situated. He appeared for the test and returned to the railway station. He went back to Pune by an express train. By 8:00 PM, he reached to Pune. He slept on his bed, as soon as he reached the guest house, where he was staying. Next morning, it was Monday. He reported to his office accordingly.

Mohan at Trishakti

Mohan was residing in Bhopal when he had to come back after resigning from Wipro Technologies Ltd. Pune, Maharashtra. Things were not so easy during his second inning in Bhopal. Now he was under expectations of others. He decided to prepare for the destiny, that time he had enough money, which he had earned as a software engineer, to continue his preparation to crack the competitive exams, in order to become a professional electrical engineer. He calculated his balance and found that there will be no problem up to the next three months and started preparation at a coaching institute in Bhopal.

Those three months passed very soon, some of the results came and those were negative. Although doors were always open from his family for any kind of support, but he didn't want to ask for economic support. As a student, one can put any demand before his parent. But as a job doer, it is very difficult to ask for money and especially when one has resigned from a job. He was bound to say, "Mom, now I am not doing the job anymore, I am preparing for something else at a coaching institute." His mother sensed the situation by hearing the language of his son on the cell phone and deposited enough money in Mohan's account, with the help of that Mohan could continue up to the next two months.

Having more than 80% in both High school and higher secondary school, having a B.Tech. Degree from one of the well-known NIT, Mohan had never imagined that his life would come to this one day. He appeared for many interviews but was rejected for the reason that he has a good academic record and a sound degree from one of the NIT. Yes, the interviewers had a great doubt that why a person, having such a good record, will work for us. The moment, he will have a good job, he will leave us. The time was in the pure opposite direction because his strengths were the main cause of his rejection. All his efforts turned to dust. But he was firm in his decision to do a job, related to the field of electrical technology or he won't accept the job.

Meanwhile, he got some calls from software industries, including a call from Accurem Technologies Ltd. but Mohan didn't accept those. The calls from software industries were of no meaning for Mohan.

One day Mohan sat alone and recollected some memories when he had presented his strengths and won over the moments. "But today, why is all that not possible?" Mohan said to himself. Then he started to think, what he had today to give others, to serve for and to get paid, having a condition that he will serve in the field of electrical technology only because he had a degree in that special field. He prepared his latest resume and posted that to some core companies based on electrical technology and also sent the resume to some reputed institutes for the post of a lecturer. He got some calls from some companies, but no offer fitted his expectations.

Mohan had no option and then he visited his alma mater, where he had completed his degree and explained about his present situation before the director sir himself. The director sir ensured to do something in favor of him. The matter was solved internally within the college in Mohan's favor. Mohan got the call just another day to report there at college for an official interview.

"Don't worry Mohan, we have a vacant post of Research Associate in this very department, which you want to work in. We hope that there would be required progress in the project with your presence now, so your position is confirmed. Now as far as the joining is concerned, since there would be some paperwork regarding your joining, you need to wait for about a week in order to get an official offer letter for the post, meanwhile you are welcome from tomorrow itself, if you are willing to know about the project," The interviewer said. "Thank you very much Sir, I shall wait for an official response," Mohan replied.

Part-II

He was waiting very eagerly for the official response from NIT. Five days passed. On the evening of 6th day, when he was roaming around the new market near Top n Town; he got a call from an engineering institute. "Hello, may I talk to Mr. Mohan," it was such a lovely and sweet voice of a female at the other end. "Yes, Madam, Mohan is talking," he replied. "Mr. Mohan, you had applied for the post of a lecturer in electrical department at Trishakti Institute of Technology & Research, your interview for the post, is scheduled on 6 PM tomorrow at our corporate office, that is in Kasturba Nagar, near *Chetak Bridge*, will it be convenient for you to attend the interview at the mentioned venue?" The lady asked. Mohan was lost somewhere, he was not sure about what should he reply. Because he was 99% sure about joining the post of research associate at the NIT, he was just waiting for the offer letter from there. But what a lovely voice that was!! He tried to prolong the conversation, although he got it but asked again, "Madam, could you please tell me about the address of the venue again?"

"Yes, sure" the lady replied. And she explained very nicely that he again forgot later on.

"Madam, May I know your name please?" Mohan asked. "Savita," She replied.

"Thanks, Savita, I shall see you tomorrow evening at the venue."

"Sure sir," She replied and cut the phone.

"Whether I join it or not; but one thing is sure that I am going to appear for the interview," Mohan thought, smiled and went back to home.

Next morning, he turned pages from some of the books to prepare for some basic concepts of Basic Electrical Engineering and Network Analysis etc. At the right time, he reached the venue, he managed to reach there using some friend's contacts because he had already forgotten the address of the corporate office. He rushed to the reception to know whether he is at the right building or not. The lady at the reception asked, "Yes sir, how can I help you?" Mohan didn't reply anything. Instead, he asked, "Are you Savita?" "Yes sir, I had called you yesterday, "She replied. And she explained to him about his turn for the interview. Mohan waited till then. After some time he heard, "Who is Mr. Mohan? You have to go to that room for an interview." "Thank you," Mohan replied. When his turn came, he rushed there. The four big personalities, the vice-chairman, the secretary, the advisor and the director sir were waiting for him there. "May I come in sir? "Mohan asked. And the historical interview happened.

He was still waiting for the response from NIT and of course, was eager to know at least the result of the interview, which was held on last Saturday. There were two options now, but no one was 100% clear. He decided to join the institute from where he will get the call first.

On Monday his cell phone rang, he picked up. "Congratulation Mohan, you are selected for the post and you are required to report on Tuesday morning 9 AM at the institute building," Deepak sir, one of the existing faculty of the institute informed to Mohan. "Thank you sir, I shall report on Tuesday," Mohan replied.

Same day Mohan checked his email in the evening and saw the offer letter from NIT for the post of a Research Associate. Now he was in a dilemma, the debate began in his mind, NIT or TRISHAKTI? Government institute or Private institute? Research Associate or Lecturer? Working on a project or Teaching the students? There were many times in his life when he came across the same situations to choose one between two. So as usual to discuss the matter, he called his mother and explained the situation. His mother asked, "What do you want to join?"

"I am still in confused, that's why I called you," Mohan replied.

"Then you can go for the one, from where you got the call first".

"Thanks Mom," He replied and cut the phone. He thought for some time and chose the Trishakti Institute.

Once Mohan had willed to become a teacher but he had never imagined that the wish will get fulfilled in this way. At the Trishakti Campus, he enjoyed teaching and met well-known personalities, learned a lot about teaching methodologies, management skills. He met with 240 new friends and shared his knowledge with them. Also, he was getting prepared to play the next part.

Part C
Free Thoughts

The Maya

The *Maya* is a formality in itself. It is the biggest illusion created by the creator. Nobody can remain untouched from the illusion and according to some *Hindu* religious books. Even the so-called God, who is said to be a combination of three forms; the generator, the operator and the destroyer, is affected by the *Maha-Maya* created by the almighty.

Now it won't be in our favor to treat God and the almighty differently. We must see them as one. The God is almighty and the almighty is God. It will dilute the strength of our problem to solve the mystery of illusion. We have to believe in "*sabka malik ek*" theory, of course, we can call him by different names according to the need, but we need to mix this theory in our blood that the supreme is the one only.

Now if you want to get rid of the *Maya,* forget it, it's not possible at least being alive and I can't say after that. Because every task we do, every thought we think, all are affected by the *Maya,* and even to know about the *Maya* is affected with the same. But yes, it can be easily understood in a way.

Now the very core thing about the *Maya that* we need to know is that it's not our enemy, it's just a platform to perform. You say that poverty is due to the *Maya,* then don't forget, prosperity is also due to the *Maya* itself. From centuries, people are giving credit of their success to themselves only while on suffering, they blame the *Maya* or the creator of the *Maya,* the almighty. So we need to change our mindset about the *Maya,* that the illusion of it is neutral in nature.

The *Maya* can be easily understood by keeping ourselves separate from it. And how can it be possible? Yes, it is possible by being a silent viewer, by not putting any interest or business in the thing what we see. If you enjoy the performance, it means you are entertaining yourself, just like you watch movies or listen to music. Don't forget that to get entertained is also an action and if you were in action, it means that you were affected by the *Maya.* I know it is not an easy task to remove our interest from the things happening around us. But if you want to understand what the *Maya* is, then you need to practice like this.

Just for some time, say five minutes, you forget yourself, your every character, name designation and everything. Just remember that you are only a creature who can only see, and breathing is a natural process that will keep you alive, even don't pay attention on breathing. Your nose will draw enough oxygen from the environment according to the necessity. Only become a silent viewer. Yes, you can use your body according to bodily action to remain in comfort but according to the will of the body, not according to you. You just keep your eyes open. And don't even think that these are your eyes; somehow you are able to see the scenario in front of you. You just see, being a silent watcher, without any interest, any business.

You will see that someone is celebrating, he is happy, he might be giving a party to his friends. Same time another one is sitting alone in a park nearby on a bench, he is sad because he has lost something very important to him. Nobody is with him, just for some time, one or two people come and after discussing the matter with him, saying that they are with him, making him understand, they also go.

Now return to your original state, on realizing the incident, you have found that somebody is happy and another one is sad. Yes, they both are affected by the *Maya.* But since you have not put your interest in the incident, you were only a viewer, you neither were happy with the previous one nor were sad with the later one. You were only viewing the scene. it means you were not affected by the *Maya* for those moments.

It's human nature to be happy or sad at times, but by controlling these emotions, we can make our life more beautiful, more meaningful, and more interesting. Every moment is precious, we can save a lot of time by not wasting it, celebrating the ups and crying for the downs and utilizing the time to think and work in a way to grow up, to make progress.

Knowing only and understanding the *Maya* is not sufficient. To work in a way to reduce its effect is necessary too and working on the "go ahead" theory will make you win half the battle. So the moment, we solve one mystery, we should engage ourselves in solving another because life is too short and there are infinite mysteries in the universe to solve.

Religion

A path on which you move; a willingness through which you start a passion, which reminds you; a group of rules which you follow in order to know and understand the supernatural universe and the very creator of it, the supreme.

Every creature of the universe is unique in itself. It is not necessary that the religion of all the creatures must be the same. Everyone has the freedom to define and practice their own religion, keeping in mind that their practice must not become the cause of disturbance for other's freedom and their religion.

Intelligent ones did so and those were also successful in knowing the almighty and his very way of running the world. They never said that people should follow them. They only said that people should follow the truth and honesty. They might have helped the people in defining people's individual religions, but nobody was interested in asking for help. All were only interested in knowing the religions of those great ones. Nobody wanted to do the journey in depth.

People want to attain the whole, just by reading some predefined religious books, chanting some predefined religious words, It's just not possible. They may only know that God is kind like that. But they can't feel it just by doing so.

Some pupils were much disciplined, they were also successful in attaining the things up to maximum possible instinct, but not fully. Because they were continuously holding the finger of their masters even in last moments. None of the efforts was original. And the journey won't be complete until one is original. Now what is the point of going through this journey, if it is not completed till its last moments?

Enlightened ones make a direct conversation with the whole. They will never tell you that God is like this, God is like that. They will make you feel God, provided your will is there.

I am not asking to avoid all this. I am just saying that don't stop here. Keep moving till the miracle happens. Otherwise, don't waste your time. The incomplete journey will be of no worth, it will only create more and more confusions.

Read scientific and religious books, Attain the company of great people and enlightened ones. You will be inspired by doing so. And let their views be the cause of roots of your own religion. But don't agree with the things, which your heart doesn't want to accept.

This is not a problem in the case of the enlightened ones, because they take care of it all. They'll never force their belief, which may cause any obstacle in your journey. They will only tell the things which are necessary for you. Therefore the enlightened ones can be the perfect "Gurus." But in the case of other religious people, especially when you are reading books, you need to be very attentive, very cautioned.

Religion is those 99 steps, on which you move after a call from the supernatural power, the supreme. You just need to take the very first step on your own. And that is your willingness to move.

The answers are already there, scattered here and there in our universe. But those answers are waiting for their questions, which are to be asked by you. Ask as many questions as possible by heart. Ask from the bottom of your heart- "Oh God, who are you? Who am I? What's my destination in this world?" And the butterflies of answers will start converging towards you. You will find those answers in some form for sure.

The basic things of each existing religion are more or less, same. All agree that the supreme is one. And the founders of other religions have been accepted as great people by any other religion.

As your eternal journey will start, you will start loving your parents and friends a lot. Because now you'll be able to feel the power of God in them, yes, they are a form of the god only. As you'll move forward, you'll be able to see the form of god in many people. You'll not only know it because it may be written in some books or you've read here, but you'll be able to feel it. You'll go through many experiences and will feel the very presence and will of God everywhere.

Your every step, which is in favor of those 99 steps, is your religion now. And whatever obstacle you come through in your way, you have to overcome that. You just need to have the willingness to overcome and the things will turn in your favor dramatically. You'll understand and feel more and more the existence of some power around you, after every such incident.

Then you can be assured of your journey has begun now.

Questions and Answers

Q. 1. What drives you to write?

A. Nature, family, friends, society; these all. One must have some way to express oneself. As Aristotle says, "Human is a social animal." We can't imagine ourselves being alone, happy and capable of all. Living and sharing our knowledge, earning and experiences with other people, make us feel that we are well connected with others. Sharing has some eternal positivity in itself. That's why if we share our sorrow, it gets diminished and while sharing our joy, it gets enhanced. Sharing my thoughts and experiences with readers makes me feel like being a part of a big joint family, called *Vasudha*. As they say-"*vasudhaiv kutumbakam*." The whole earth is a family.

Q. 2. Define GOD.

A. When I was about seven years old, I had asked the same question to my grandpa in a little bit different sense. I had asked, "Who is GOD?" I had a strong reason to ask this question. And the reason was that I knew almost all the people I had heard about, except GOD. My grandpa didn't get astonished with my question. He simply replied, "GOD is a power which is responsible to run the whole universe, a power which is responsible for all." I accepted this and I believe in it. Now you have asked about definition. So better, you should ask the definition of power. And the answer is written in science books, that the capacity to do work is called power. It's simple, I believe.

Q. 3. Is it really so simple, to understand the GOD?

A. If you can understand a human being, you can understand GOD. The only difference is that both lie in different sets of dimensions. If you want to understand a person, you will surely need to think according to his/her perception, otherwise using just your perception will not serve the purpose. One can't see the whole map on a globe at a time. To do so, one either needs to turn the globe or himself. So, to understand GOD too, one needs to think from GOD's perspective.

Q. 4. And what is GOD's perspective?

A. This you should ask yourself. Then only the answer will be justified. Otherwise, it will have no meaning, no joy and no satisfaction. Create your own world, write your own story and then ask from yourself, how important you are, for your created world? How important role you are playing in your written story. The answers, which you will get in return, will change your attitude forever. You will be a different you then. But this practice, you need to do it on your own.

Q. 5. How do you find the art that can help us to know self and supreme?

A. Art is doing something original, following and exploring your own vision. It gives you a bliss feeling. When you perform something in your own way, then your own hidden power helps you to perform. These hidden powers are your intellect, prudent, will and imagination. Otherwise just copying others doesn't need these powers. Anybody can copy. But the originals are very few.

Once, in a classroom, the teacher asked his students to write an application for leave. The students, who were weak in studies or the students who didn't want to use their mind, just copied the application from the nearest source possible. Assignments were submitted. When the teacher checked their applications, he caught the poor students, who copied, because those students copied the name and signature also.

Art is a signature of the supreme self through his creatures. When you put your signature on paper, remember, it's your own property. Nobody has taught you to sign. It's your own creation. For the first time, when you signed, you were helped by you only. You drew something similar to your name. Your inner power helped you. Supreme power helped you. And your inner power and supreme power are not different. These are well connected to each other. Stepping towards your own way means you are finding a new way; a new creation is going to happen. It's an art. And in the moments of creation, you enjoy your being; you enjoy the glimpse of supreme.

Q. 6. You said, "Glimpse of supreme". What if somebody is not satisfied with the glimpse; somebody wants more and more?

A. That's a good sign. One shouldn't get satisfied with the glimpse only. But those glimpses increase the thirst to go in more depth. It's natural. Keep continuing towards your own path, it will lead you to get more and more.

Q. 7. But what's the limit? Up to when should somebody keep moving?

A. The sky is the limit if you are following airway. The surface under the deep sea is the limit, If you are following waterway. (Smiles) One must accept the fact that a drop can't experience an ocean. It can only imagine. In physical science, if some number or something is one million times bigger than another.

Then it is termed as infinity with respect to the smaller one. Can you imagine how many times; is the sea bigger than a drop? Infinity is a relative term in physical science. Drop is part and parcel of the sea. The drop has its own limitations. It can't take a whale inside it. It can only imagine in that way. Art is a journey. One reaches a new stage after every milestone. An artist never gets satisfied with his work. An artist never stops. But somewhere in the midst, a miracle happens. GOD's perspective awakens in him. At the moment, one understands that behind the whole, there is power. He becomes kind to others. Because he sees the same part in others too, what he has felt in himself. Then he starts thinking and doing things for the benefits of the whole. All have their own experiences.